PENGUIN BOOKS
THE BURDEN OF DEMOCRACY

Pratap Bhanu Mehta is an Indian academic. He has been the president of the Centre for Policy Research and has taught at New York University, Harvard University and Jawaharlal Nehru University. Since July 2017, he is the vice chancellor of Ashoka University. His areas of research include political theory, constitutional law, society and politics in India, governance and political economy, and international affairs. Mehta has served on many central government committees, including India's National Security Advisory Board, the Prime Minister of India's National Knowledge Commission, and a Supreme Court–appointed committee on elections in Indian universities. He received the 2010 Malcom S. Adisheshiah Award and the 2011 Infosys Prize for Social Sciences.

THE

BURDEN

OF

DEMOCRACY

PRATAP BHANU MEHTA

PENGUIN BOOKS

An imprint of Penguin Random House

PENGUIN BOOKS

USA | Canada | UK | Ireland | Australia
New Zealand | India | South Africa | China | Singapore

Penguin Books is part of the Penguin Random House group of companies
whose addresses can be found at global.penguinrandomhouse.com

Published by Penguin Random House India Pvt. Ltd
4th Floor, Capital Tower 1, MG Road,
Gurugram 122 002, Haryana, India

Penguin
Random House
India

First published by Penguin Books India 2003

ISBN 9780143441038

Typeset in Times New Roman by Manipal Digital Systems, Manipal
Printed at Manipal Technologies Limited, India

www.penguin.co.in

It's better . . .
To honour Equality who ties friends to
friends, cities to cities, allies to allies.
For equality is stable among men.
If not the lesser hates the greater force,
And so begins the day of enmity.
Equality set up men's weights and
measures, Gave them their numbers.

—Euripides, *The Phoenician Women*

AUTHOR'S NOTE

To write a short essay on Indian democracy is an enterprise fraught with difficulty. This is not simply because the subject is too vast, complex and not yet fully fathomed to be ripe for synoptic treatment. It is rather that finding the right register with which to convey this complexity is an enormously delicate task. An assessment of India's successes too easily shades over into an uncritical self-congratulation; a critique of the failures and depredations of Indian democracy on the other hand often borders on the misanthropic. Misplaced hope in the democratic experiment can easily turn into self-delusion; on the other hand, the line between realism and outright cynicism is very thin. The very contrariness of the emotions that the Indian democratic experience evokes alternate wonder and horror at the same time; the very diverse social facts that it contains make keeping the storyline always under control, always adequate to the reality being described that much more difficult. There are many good books written on facets of the Indian political scenario, but anyone who seriously negotiates its complexity cannot but help admitting that contradicting oneself or feeling tentative cannot be avoided if one knows India too well.

This prefatory remark is simply by way of a warning that what follows is neither comprehensive—it leaves out many important topics, including the question of the relationship between nationalism and democracy—nor is it the only plausible story that can be told about India's democratic experience. I do not believe the patently debilitating thought that therefore any story is as good as the other. But I do believe that the plausibility of any story will in turn depend upon how it resonates with a particular reader's knowledge and experience. This essay is not a work of social science in the conventional sense of the term. It highlights particular features of India's democratic experience that I take to be significant but somewhat more elusive. The aim of the essay is to hopefully enlighten, but not instruct; those looking for 'solutions' will be disappointed. But if there is a single thread running through this essay, it is this: the ideological persistence of social inequality on the one hand and a mistaken view of the state's proper function and organization on the other have modified and impeded the workings of democracy and its effects in all kinds of perverse ways.

Both of these will need to be addressed, but doing so will require not just confronting the rough and tumble of Indian politics, but also recovering a profound sense of what democracy is all about, and a new ideological imagination that can contextualize and throw light on our discontents. This task will be laborious in every sense of the word, but the romance of democracy has also to be accompanied by *political* hard work, and politics, in its highest form, is nothing if not hard.

Introduction

The creation of India as a sovereign independent republic was, in some profound sense, the commencement of a bold experiment in political affairs as significant as any that had been conducted in history. To give 200 million largely unlettered and unpropertied people the right to choose their own government, and the attendant freedoms that come with it, was a leap of faith for which there was no precedent in human history. Certainly, no body of European social thinking at the time, on the prospects of democracy, would have counselled such a course; there was no instance from the past that could be the basis for confidence that this experiment would work. No political formation that could provide an instructive example of how to make democracy work in such seemingly unpropitious circumstances: unbounded poverty, illiteracy, the absence of a middle class and immense and deeply entrenched social cleavages. Indeed, if history and social theory were taken to be any guide, the presumption would have been quite the reverse. Democracy in India is a phenomenon that, by most accounts, should not have existed, flourished or, indeed, long endured.

What does democracy mean in this setting apart from its obvious reference to practices of popular authorization? Can one fix the meaning of 'democracy', the hopes and aspirations it generated, in a setting as socially diverse as India's? Democracy would mean hope; it would establish the principle of political equality, freedom and dignity indelibly in Indian society. But what concrete sense of empowerment and opportunity would it bring to bonded labour, landless peasantry, deprived untouchables? Could they share the same expectations from democracy, and all the liberal freedoms that came with it as, say, their middle-class lawyer counterparts who drew up the Constitution? Despite some limited experience with self-government, there was no way knowing what possessing the right to vote meant, or how indeed it would be exercised. For some, democracy would appear to mean the freedom to rediscover and assert their tradition, for others, protection from it. What new forms of collective mobilization would democracy bring about and what ends would these serve? The kaleidoscope of meanings, expectations and hopes that different sections of Indian society placed on democracy, the various ways in which they contextualized it, would render any attempt to fix its meaning and scope futile. The symbols of a new awakening India, the flag, the ubiquitous presence of Nehru—in whose own figure most expected the contradictions of India to resolve themselves, the Congress party—that had for the most part and brilliantly engineered a multi-class, multiregional alliance, all symbolized immense hope, but one whose contents remained undefined and contested. Many groups would try to redeem the promissory note that the republican constitution promised in their own distinctive and often conflictual ways. The protean character and meaning of India's democracy would occasion the remark that the point of democracy is to be forever a contest over its own meaning.

The significance of India's democratic experiment was itself disguised by the historical process through which it came about. While there was a good deal of consensus, even as early as the beginning of the twentieth century, that 'the people' would in some senses be authoritative, there was also a lot of confusion over what exact form the deference to popular sovereignty would take. As it happened, representative institutions slowly took shape as an outcome of the nationalist movement's struggle against the colonial powers. The early experiments in representative government were limited both by the extent of suffrage and the scope of the powers allotted to those governments that worked under them. But representative government came to be characterized as simply the outcome of a negotiation between India's elites on the one hand, and colonial powers on the other. Democracy, on this view, was not the object of ideological passion, it was not born of a deep sense of conviction widely shared, but it was simply the contingent outcome of the conflicts amongst India's different elites, or an unintended by-product of the British having produced too many lawyers adept in the idioms of modern politics. There was no grand design in Indian democracy, and hence nothing to memorialize in the way the American and French revolutions did their democratic transitions.

Secondly, there was the obvious fact that nationalism, rather than democracy, seemed to be a more primary political passion. While the two are by no means incompatible, it was unclear to many whether the great churning the nationalist movement had produced was sustained by the primacy of the nation or a love of democracy. The celebration of a nation that had ostensibly existed since time immemorial seems to disguise the fact that something radically new was happening. The nation seemed to then, as it often does now, cast a shadow over the democracy that ought to define it, and the trauma of Partition seemed to make the momentous deliberations of the Constituent Assembly appear trite.

The invention of republican citizenship in India was indeed a historic event, and a rupture with the past. While many had hoped that the new constitution would simply be encased within the supposed historical identity of India, its diverse and complex cultural sympathies, few imagined that the opportunities it afforded would intensely politicize all areas of organized collective existence in India. The resources of history and culture, rather than providing comfort and continuity, would themselves be the first categories to be subject to intense political scrutiny. The nationalist movement had attempted the delicate task of making India transcend its own traditions without making tradition itself despicable; to repose a faith in an Indian identity that could survive the contested character of its political expressions. But in the end, democratic politics was the space where the place of tradition and the question of identity alike would be reopened.

Then there was disavowed continuity with the colonial state. If the faith reposed in democracy was unique to India, the style in which government was imagined was anything but. The entire colonial state apparatus, with its laws, conventions, ubiquitous rules, faith in the impartiality of the few good men that comprised the state, was taken over almost intact. To be sure, the state was now to be used for nationalist ends, to secure India's territorial integrity, to spread and implement the development mission of the new regime. But the relationship between this state apparatus, to whatever ends it was going to be deployed, and democracy was going to forever remain contentious. Indian democracy was going to make this state apparatus its own, put the imprimatur of its social conflicts upon it, yet at the same time it would continue to disavow it as distant, undemocratic and even colonial. But whether housed in a state that looked more traditional than it claimed to be, or in a tradition that looked more modern than it admitted to being, the simple fact was that for the first time in Indian history, all Indians were declared to be citizens, not subjects. Whether or not republics had existed in ancient India, whether or not democracy had cultural roots in 1951, was of less concern. As citizens, people would not only enjoy rights, but exercise *choice*, a choice to make and remake the social world in accordance with their will.

It would not be an overstatement to see the tumult of Indian politics as that of people exercising these choices vigorously. The matter of choice is basic to the debate over Indian democracy today. The debate over Indian democracy essentially may be boiled down to two key questions related to choices. Is the idea of exercising political choice itself a meaningful claim, or is it simply an illusion? And if it is a meaningful claim, has the exercise of political choices by citizens, the use of opportunities that political democracy affords, led to the creation of a better social world? This essay, especially sections two and three, look at the ways in which the experience of inequality and the workings of the Indian state have a bearing on these questions. It assumes that the idea of citizens trying to remake their social world is not entirely an illusion. But our choices have come to bear the imprint of the social inequality on the one hand, and an overbearing statism on the other. It argues that the texture of social relations in Indian society deforms its politics, and that the organization of the state impedes it from serving us well. In some ways, these two claims are very obvious and well recognized. What I think is less well recognized is this: that inequality and our relations to the state are not simply structural injustices, they also profoundly shape our sense of self and its social possibilities. It is the peculiar sense of the self in relation to others that social inequality and the state have produced that gives Indian politics its texture. This account is, if you like, as much 'moral-psychological', as it is structural. But I hope it will pick out the deeper senses in which we remain discontented with our democracy.

Universal adult suffrage was going to have social implications far beyond its immediate political significance. As one of the most thoughtful commentators of the time, K.M. Panikkar, put it, 'Many social groups previously unaware of their strength, and barely touched by the political changes that had taken place, suddenly realized that they were in a position to wield power.' The right to participate in choosing one's electors was the most dramatic way of affirming the equality of all citizens. Although the right to vote is seen by many as a meagre right, whose exercise is a periodic ritual that does little to enhance the well-being of those who exercise it, the right itself transforms the meaning of social existence. It is an assertion that all authority is a conditional grant, that suffrage establishes the sufferance, as George Kateb so eloquently put it. Democracy, as its earliest observers were quick to note, represents the dissolution of inherited modes of authority, indeed of the whole concept of authority itself. Once instituted, democracy is an incitement to politicize all areas of social life; it introduces, over time, a process of critique that questions and subverts all certainties of social life. The very mundane process of seeking majorities within a representative system, of building new coalitions, leads to the mobilization of new groups, unsettles existing power equations and produces new openings.

The process of democratization will thus always produce radical uncertainty about authority and identity alike. As the legitimacy of old ways of instituting authority and recognizing identities dissolves, without being replaced by new norms and conventions, the experience of democracy will be profoundly confusing. As Alexis de Tocqueville put it incomparably:

> Obedience, then loses moral basis in the eyes of him who obeys; he no longer considers it as a divinely appointed duty; and he does not yet see its purely human aspect; in his eyes it is neither sacred nor just and he submits to it as a degrading though useful fact. There is an unspoken intestinal power between permanently suspicious rival powers. The lines between authority and tyranny, liberty and licence, right and might seem so jumbled and confused that no one knows exactly what he is, what he can do and what he should do.

The experience of democracy in India has opened up numerous points of dissent, new conflicts of values and identities, a permanent antagonism of meaning and interest that leaves its citizens often with an overwhelming sense that Indian society is flying off in many different directions at once and the unity of all reference points seems to vanish. There is what might, at a high level of abstraction, be defined as a commitment to democratic procedures—free elections, free press,

9

basic set of liberal rights such as freedom of expression (often frayed at the edges)—but the point of all these is subject to contending interpretations.

In some ways, this dissolution of convictions and the conflicts that democracy has provoked are part of a process of deeper democratization. Ironically, new bonds have been created through the process of social antagonism itself, and through the process of argument, a new shared public is being created. Different groups may not share the same viewpoints but there is a sense in which the audiences they are beginning to address to secure their power are increasingly shared. Groups may have deep-seated grievances and suppressed complexes but the mere freedom to articulate them gives them a stake in the system like nothing else does. And the imperatives of seeking sustainable majorities, most observers argue, moderate even the most radical of movements, giving Indian politics a largely centrist cast. Indeed, there is a palpable sense in which the following claim is true. Take for instance the complex issues raised by regional identities in India. Whenever India has tried democratic accommodation, it has succeeded. State subverting ethnic violence, in places like Punjab and Kashmir, has invariably been fuelled by the authoritarian moments in the Indian state. Indeed, democracy's biggest triumph is that it has proven to be an effective—perhaps the only—mechanism for holding India together. It is true that one of the reasons for the relative success of its democracy, and its hanging together as a nation, has been the profoundly cross-cutting character of cleavages within Indian society that has made collective action on a large scale, to overthrow the state, quite difficult to mount. But democracy has both brought out conflicts into the open and provided an effective mechanism for accommodating them. India has worked not because of 'unity in diversity', the presence of a locus of identity beneath differences, as the state is fond of telling us. We have flourished rather because we are 'diverse in our unities', each able to imagine the connection with others in his/her own way. Of course, the success of democracy in carving a nation is not overdetermined by the presence of democracy alone and it would be foolish to underestimate the role of creative political choices—the linguistic reorganization of states, for example. But conflict is a way of getting different groups to participate, to give them a stake in a manner that suggests that despite tumultuous conflict, there is an immense process of incorporation of hitherto excluded groups going on.

Despite this plausible story of Indian democracy as a nation come to life through a million mutinies, to use Naipaul's phrase, most assessments of Indian democracy are far more ambivalent. On the one hand, there is what might be called the optimistic narrative of deepening. On this view, Indian democracy is producing an ever-greater politicization of social relationships; the discourses of equality and the assertion of agency are pervading more areas of social life; impressive voter turnouts, especially amongst the poor and dispossessed, suggest that democracy has a wider social basis—in particular, its resonance is even greater for non-middle classes. The enormous fluidity in the political structure, the constant rise of new social groups, the high turnover of incumbents and governments alike, the intensification of social struggle, the rising consciousness of rights—these are all testimony not only to the success of this experiment but its deepening. Even if democracy, as practised today, has not allowed as spectacular an amelioration of our material conditions as we had hoped, it has at least managed to avoid catastrophes such as mass starvation. Even though progress in India's democracy might be slow—subject to the vicissitudes of a million negotiations—at least it has laid the foundation for more enduring and inclusive success. And then there is the sheer romance of Indian democracy, its capacity to generate so much argument and energy and conduct politics on such a mammoth scale. The diversity and contradictions it has produced make perhaps Plato's claim that a democracy will contain 'a complete assortment of constitutions' within it, truer of India than any place else.

On the other hand, there is the grim narrative of decline, or at least crisis. This narrative focuses on the alarming character of the present conjuncture. Democratic mobilization, while it has produced an intense struggle for power, has not delivered millions of citizens from the abject dictates of poverty. Yes, the broad framework within which practices of popular authorization can be carried out remain intact, but politics itself has become an area where norms exist only in their breach. India is proving, it seems, to use Burke's powerful formulation that 'forms of a free and the ends of an arbitrary government are proving to be things not altogether incompatible'. The very mechanism, designed to secure the liberty, well-being and dignity of citizens, representative democracy, is routinely throwing up forces that threaten to undermine it; the very laws that are supposed to enshrine republican aspirations are incapable of commanding minimal respect, and their inaction subjects the entire political process to ridicule. The corruption, mediocrity, indiscipline, venality and lack of moral imagination of the political class, those essential agents of representation in any democracy, makes them incapable of attending to the well-being of citizens. The capture of the political process, by the meanest of interests, intermittently violent, occasionally unleashing uncontrollable passions, the lack of any ideological coherence, all suggest democracy has become a hollow shell. It is a ritual, albeit an engaging and spectacular one, that is inhibiting our liberties and well-being alike. The best thing we can say about the forces it has generated, to borrow a line from Yeats, is: 'The best lack all conviction, while the worst are full of passionate intensity.'

It would be a rare citizen who has not felt the force of both narratives directly. The difficult question is how to bring the two together. There is one simple way of connecting them. This is the thought that excess of political mobilization has placed such an enormous strain on Indian institutions, to the point that they have been rendered dysfunctional, producing a crisis of governability. The clamour of so many, and often incompatible demands at once makes it impossible for the state to make anyone happy. This story is plausible, but in the end, profoundly misleading because the sources of the 'crisis of governability' are many and most of them have nothing to do with excess of mobilization.

Continued concentrations of power, institutions and mechanisms of control designed with ever-perverse incentive in mind and state action itself have contributed to this crisis a good deal. But fundamentally, it is the political choices, the daily decisions that politicians particularly, but citizens as well, make that produce a crisis. It is not structurally overdetermined but a product of the *choices* we make.

There is another narrative that appeals to a kind of inner dialectic at work amongst the conflicts in Indian democracy. It hopes that the very process of conflict and antagonism will lead to empowerment, and through that medium produce a more lasting and just politics. What we are witnessing is something more akin to a transitional stage, a process of churning of old injustices necessary to produce a politics with more credible moral convictions. Whether or not this claim is credible, only time will tell. But this narrative at least points in the right direction. Whatever the infirmities of our democracy, the greater danger lies in giving up on the project, as we are apt to do in our longing for more disciplinarian moments such as the Emergency. A contempt for politics will be worse than the corruption of politics; a search for an answer to our discontent is doomed unless it goes through the dangerous process of politics itself. This is something I firmly believe in, and for me, to be a democrat and express contempt for politics, even with its sordid horse-trading, opportunism and feverishness, is almost an oxymoron.

But at the present conjuncture, the claim that politics and the countless negotiations we are currently witnessing necessarily lead to a good and decent society appears to many simply an act of faith. Democracy's virtue, Tocqueville claimed, was that it makes 'retrievable mistakes'. That this claim is comforting only if mistakes are actually retrieved might be the cynical response, and most of us, as citizens, are perilously in that state of mind. (A lighter version of this response, also equally applicable, is Clement Atlee's retort that democracy as discussion works only if at some point people stop talking.) Unless the central paradox of the Indian democratic experience is confronted, there is no guarantee that a deep alienation will not be produced that will make Indian democracy vulnerable to damaging conflict or something worse. And the central paradox is this: The practices of popular authorization have not produced a society that is even in a minimal sense free of egregious forms of domination or gives substantial meaning to the idea of civic reciprocity.

The rest of this essay will take another starting point. This will be, to put it provocatively, that in order to love democracy well you have to love it moderately. This is not meant to be an anti-democratic thought. It would be inappropriate to complain of too much democracy in a society where most agents are still so

16

thoroughly disempowered. It is rather the thought that even if we are passionately convinced about the democratic project, even if we are convinced that the worst the people can do, when not subverted by those who claim to represent them, is to commit errors rather than crimes, we need to be more self-aware about the political choices we make, and the use of appeals to democracy as an excuse for not thinking. This is particularly true in a context where the most potent danger to the profound humanity and dignity of all individuals, that democracy was meant to honour, is coming from political movements that have adorned the mantle of democracy. The fact that a movement like Hindu nationalism can so easily rest its claim to authority by appealing to a majoritarian conception of democracy, or that so many political forces from Jayalalithaa to Bal Thackeray to Laloo Yadav can operate so successfully outside any permitted legal boundaries, suggests that somewhere, we as citizens have to come to a greater depth of agreement over the question: What *is* this democracy for? Is Indian democracy simply going to be an excuse for an unbridled and open competition, in which those who can raise their banner the highest, declaim in the loudest voices, and mobilize the maximum amount of muscle power, can make their writ run large. Will India's democracy sustain itself, if at all, not by even a dim sense of the values democracy is meant to honour, but by the sheer contingencies of power in Indian society? While Indian democracy has been successful, we cannot take it for granted that the shifting balance of power may not produce forms of state action which jeopardize and put at risk every defensible ideal to which this republic was committed.

Discussions of Indian politics suffer from a kind of over-attribution to democracy. Middle-class despair of democracy tends to blame almost every symptom of our discontent to excess democracy. In response, populists, intellectuals and others blame every ill on the lack of democracy. Both responses are unilluminating, in part because the causal story implied in both is much too simple-minded. When we praise or blame democracy, we are often like the person looking for his lost key under the lamp post, not because he has lost it there, but because it is bright there. Outcomes that are conducive to our well-being, such as better human development indicators or economic performance, are a product of a complex set of factors, and simply invoking 'democracy' as another rallying cry, without careful causal analysis, serves neither our goals nor the cause of democracy. Just as it would be a mistake to think, as I shall argue, that democracy has in some ways impeded our ability to make right policy choices, it would be a mistake to think that democracy as a rallying point would be a solution to all our ills. This simple point bears stressing because many of the genuine critiques of the Indian state that emerged during the crisis of the 1970s, such as the JP movement, and many of the intellectual glosses on them, were utterly naive and uncompromising when it came to thinking about the institutional and policy prerequisites that could make democracy more effective. Using undifferentiated appeals to the 'people' is, as we know, as much a ruse for power in a democracy as it is a solution to practical problems. No responsible thinking about democracy can avoid difficult institutional questions about how to organize power in a democratic society; and appeals to the authority of the 'people' is no substitute for a more careful thinking.

Can democracy itself generate new social norms that give its citizens some moral anchor, some intelligible and convincing sense of the proper scope of their rights and obligations vis-à-vis others, that carries some degree of conviction? Do the conflicts and uncertainties that democracy has produced run all the way down, so to speak, so that even the minimal moral restraints that are necessary for the functioning of institutions, the pacification of violence, and the norms of civility are wearing thin? The confusion between 'right and might' that Tocqueville so presciently spoke of seems to bear very heavily on most citizens. Are the norms and values that citizens, in their public conduct at any rate, genuinely consider to be authoritative constraints on their behaviour, norms that are not secured simply by the threat of violence? In India, talk of a moral crisis has become at least as pervasive as the instances of corruption that exemplify it. The moral crisis referred to has several dimensions: the impunity of politicians, the high-handedness of government, the absence of minimal reciprocity in civic life, the lurking threat of violence, the weak hold of the rule of law over all sections of society, evidenced in quotidian behaviour like violation of traffic rules, and the brazen and open encroachment of public property and much worse. Such talk of a moral crisis, or what in Indian parlance is referred to as a crisis of values, can be debilitating and tiresome. Debilitating because it is the one way in which we all express contempt for democracy itself. And tiresome because it provokes the worst kind of moralism: as if, if we all took ethics classes or listened to our preachers, everything would be all right. But despite the danger of 'talk' of a moral crisis, the fact that it is so widely experienced should be taken as a profound challenge for democracy; the perceived gap between the exercise of power and the norms that are supposed to govern it is too wide for most citizens.

Tocqueville, who remains an incomparable guide to democracy, openly wondered if democracy required moral anchors that it could not itself supply. In contrasting nineteenth-century France (which was going through an acutely unstable and corrupt period in its political history) with America (where contrary to European expectations, democracy seemed to be working), Tocqueville suggested that part of the reason for its success in America was that the latter had something of a background moral consensus, which France did not possess.

Politics in America, he argued, danced lightly on the surface only because many foundational things below it remained fixed. The mores and habits of civilization, the sense of conscience, a belief in the sanctity of the individual, a minimal sense of reciprocity (at least those who belonged to the same race), a providential deference to equality, all stemmed from sources other than the practice of democracy itself. In a sense, what we would now call America's cultural capital was a source of norms and values that not only provided an anchor with which to face the flux of politics, but also provided a sense of authoritative restraint on behaviour that societies cannot do without. Whether or not this is an accurate description of the predicament of nineteenth-century France or America is not of interest here. What is of interest is whether we need something more than the practices of electoral democracy itself to generate these norms. And if these are not generated by democracy itself, where will they come from?

The danger for a society lies in a situation where, on the one hand its politics is profoundly destabilizing, and on the other, its stock of cultural capital is either corroded or unable to provide the moral anchoring without which democratic societies cannot function. The question is this: Despite having a functioning democracy for almost five decades, does the entire repertoire of our habits and practices outside the sphere of formal politics conduce to the formation of democratic citizens with a robust sense of right and wrong, a sensitive enough social conscience, and a minimal sense of justice? This question is not meant as a piece of moral sermonizing. But the fact that it so insistently presses upon us suggests that the cultural work of morally anchoring democracy, and the norms and values associated with it, the kind of cultural work that is done by religious congregations, families, schools, and a whole other ensemble of institutions, are yet to be undertaken with any degree of seriousness.

Indeed, one could argue that most of India's effective and lived cultural inheritance, is incapable of performing this task. And it is so because this inheritance is too often tainted with past injustice and its mere invocation as a vehicle for moral improvement evokes disbelief; incapable also because culturally powerful institutions such as organized religion have had their ethical core hollowed out to the point of non-existence. Sure, many Hindus, including eminent ones in the Supreme Court declare the core of Hinduism to be democracy, but this is a monumental act of rhetorically assimilating a modern value, without in a sense an acknowledgement of the effort it takes to be a democrat. But then, where is the cultural work of creating democratic citizens actually going to be carried out? What will be the regulative moral ideals that democracy will be constrained by? Will the rough and tumble of competitive politics be enough of a school for our moral sentiments? Are we confident we can create some minimal consensus around an answer to the question: what is democracy for? There is immense reason to be pessimistic on this score, and in the next section I try and articulate what some of the aspirations of democracy might be and why it is going to be so difficult to realize them.

Hindu nationalism and all the forces that may be unleashed by it pose the second challenge. One can readily acknowledge that despite deep traditions of social pluralism, there have been many points of conflict and violence between different groups, especially the religious ones in India. It does no one any good to present Hindu–Muslim relations as either a story of intractable conflict or of seamless accommodation. These conflicts, that have complicated roots, have various sources. Since Independence, the complicities that have produced them run across many communities and political persuasions. But even in the most intense periods of conflict, there was always the sense that the realm of culture and religion lay outside the state. The state would not itself radically intervene to reconstitute these relationships. At the very least, rarely did it actively promote the marginalization of minority groups. Hindu nationalism and the rise of the BJP change all that. There is a sense in which Hindu nationalism is a deeply modernizing force, completely at peace with most of the manifestations of modernity. There is also a sense in which we have to acknowledge that many citizens feel it to be a democratizing force. It has mobilized new constituencies and has tapped into a feeling of alienation from the dominant public culture of Indian politics that many experienced; it is also one idiom in which politics is vernacularized. But it is unprecedented in that, whatever its other ambitions, it is committed to using state power to marginalize minorities, not just Muslims but Christians as well, to hold out the blackmail: assimilate on our terms or else. This has not only intensified violence in many areas, it has the potential of subverting democracy too, in every sense of the term. I do not propose to deal with 'Hindu nationalism' directly in this essay other than to suggest that the crisis of self-esteem that generates it, fuels it and gives its edge, has something to do with the failures and limitations of our larger democratic project, and unless those are addressed, Hindu nationalism will continue to gain acceptance.

The third and extraordinary challenge is this: the persistent gap between the outcomes that people expect from government and its capacity to attend to their well-being; the gap between increased demands for accountability on the one hand and their relative effectiveness on the other. There is a paradoxical manner in which we experience the state to be an instrument of our collective will (whatever that means), but find that it thwarts our agency and feeling of well-being the most. In part three, I discuss the ways in which the state is, or is not, both modified by the working of democracy and vice versa. But, these three challenges—the challenge of creating moral norms that can provide the basis for a decent society, the challenge of resisting an apocalyptic politics of self-esteem that characterizes so much of Indian politics, and the challenge of making citizens work together to produce policies that they could all freely accept—may turn out to be manifestations of one single challenge: how to create citizens bound by a sense of reciprocity. The next section discusses the impediments to creating such a citizenship.

Democracy and the Politics of Self-Respect

Democracy is, in the first instance, a way of constituting political relations such that the exercise of state power receives popular authorization. Giving popular authorization its fullest and most meaningful expression under conditions of social diversity and complexity is an enormously challenging task. But the romance of democracy—the aspirations it generates and the passions it inspires—is not limited to simply electing governments. Rather, democracy unleashes the aspiration to fundamentally reorder social relations in a completely new way. It is premised on the recognition that there is no natural source of authority that can exercise power over individuals; therefore, they are all presumptively free and equal. Their legitimate moral claims cannot be denied, or their status slighted. But this aspiration can be realized only if citizens inhabit a different kind of social world. At the very minimum, this world will have the following features. First, the mode of governance in that society will routinely have to produce policies and justifications that most citizens could freely accept. Governance will have to be experienced as a less distant, arbitrary and unfair imposition of power. Second, citizens inhabit a world where they feel, to some degree, at home. This is a social world where their moral status is acknowledged, a world which is structured to enable their freedom and serve their interests—in short, a world whose modes of interaction they can call their own. Third, such a social world can be realized only if citizens recognize the good of civic friendship. They associate with each other, not only as competitors but in a relationship of reciprocal recognition and mutual respect. We can belong to this social world only if we look upon other citizens in a particular way, not simply as fodder to be always taken advantage of. These conditions, taken together, constitute the fulfilment of democratic aspirations. Only then can we say that we inhabit a social world where we can genuinely claim minimal control over the circumstances of our own lives. Only then can the *meaning* of democracy be redeemed.

The great discontent of Indian democracy is that while the practices of popular authorization, elections, public discussion and so forth are deeply entrenched and have often chastened the exercise of power, we are far from producing modes of governance that we could freely accept. Any story about why democracy as a political practice has not produced an ideal social world would be necessarily a complex one. There are some inherent institutional difficulties in translating popular aspirations into effective social outcomes.

But, I shall argue below, it is the texture of social relations in the Indian society that fundamentally thwarts us from realizing the goods of democracy. In any society, especially democratic ones, the meaning and scope of equality will be fiercely contested and will be the basis for ideological divisions. The variety of structures, caste, class and patriarchy, that maintain and reproduce inequality, are all too familiar, and the Indian society exemplifies many of these to an unconscionable degree. But in all our social and political relationships, procedures, habits of thought, patterns of conduct, the influence of inequality is palpable. And inequality is not simply a structural condition in which people find themselves, a condition measured by such objective indicators as Gini coefficients or development indices. Inequality is resented, and becomes salient for politics, because it is experienced as an existential burden that inflicts complex psychic costs by diminishing a sense of self. Not all forms of inequality are unjust, but the ways in which it shapes the self, of privileged and marginalized alike, is a complex subject. In fact, fundamentally, inequality imposes the profoundest burdens when it is seen as denying individuals the minimum regard due to them, or when it constantly puts them in situations that are humiliating. It leaves an indelible mark on the texture of all social relations and political processes; its shadow is felt even in the most unexpected places. It remains not only one of the biggest 'burden' of democracy, it is, I shall argue, an *explanation* for many of our discontents as well.

It is now a commonplace observation, thanks largely to Rousseau who most vividly wrote about the psychic burdens of inequality, that most human beings, unless they have been dehumanized to an unimaginable degree, place some value upon themselves. This does not mean that they are selfish; it is rather that they place some *value* upon themselves and wish that this be somewhere affirmed. The institutions and practices of most inegalitarian societies deny individuals this basic form of recognition—that they are valuable in some sense, that they have some moral standing. In such societies, the quest for having one's worth affirmed will take a debased form. The only way in which one can secure the acknowledgement of others is either by seeking to dominate them, or by putting a convincing show of attributes and accomplishments, by being able to say, 'I know I am worth something because I have power over you.' Those not in a position of being able to do so adopt other more self-debasing ways. They say something like, 'Pay attention to me, because I can make your comparative sense of self-worth even more pronounced by debasing my self for you, by flattering you.' Inegalitarian societies, where there is no public acknowledgement of individual self-worth, will be characterized by both a fierce competition to dominate, and paradoxically, an exaggerated sense of servility. These are the two main strategies. Both, a desire to dominate and a kind of self-abasement, Rousseau suggested, would cause us to lead inauthentic lives: lives that were not governed by values and concerns that were properly our own. Such societies would also give individuals frequent reasons to consider their self-respect injured: inegalitarian societies will routinely humiliate its members.

The desire for democracy is in part a desire to have one's moral worth acknowledged. The charge that an arrangement or a set of procedures is 'undemocratic' is accompanied by the sentiment that lack of democracy is an affront because it slights someone's moral standing. Recognition by others of your moral worth is at least partly constitutive of an individual's feeling of self-respect, which is necessary to have a firm sense of one's own value, to have the conviction not only that life is worth living but worth living well. Its absence can be corrosive; it can make most pursuits meaningless.

In some respects, equal voting rights are a dramatic expression of any individual's moral worth. And the democratic conception of the right of all individuals, as members of society, to the full life and free development of which they are capable, is the most potent form of this recognition. But unless the collective arrangements of society give individuals the minimum bases for social self-respect, of which the equal right to vote is just one aspect, it is likely to be characterized by the aforementioned combination of a fierce competition for domination and abject servility, and when neither succeeds, violence as a way of announcing one's power and standing. What institutions and objectives best satisfy the minimal requirements of acknowledging people's moral worth is a debatable one. But at the very least, these institutions ought to secure freedom from basic necessities, removal of invidious and humiliating forms of discrimination, some equality of opportunity and access to a set of goods that are essential for being a capable agent in the modern world. The great liberal hope, embodied in the Indian Constitution, was that ameliorating serious material deprivation and achieving an effective equal standing in the eyes of the law would go some way towards mitigating the just desire to have one's worth affirmed. In doing so, it would mitigate the impulse to seek recognition either by dominating others, or by having one's own sense of self fashioned by what we think might get others' attention. Indeed, arguably, if the basis for social self-respect of all citizens is adequately protected, the existence of other inequalities might matter less, because they could not be used as a base from which to dominate, despise or negate others. Under conditions where your self-respect is not thwarted and all essential opportunities are made available to you, inequality of talent or wealth would probably matter less to you than in conditions where these impinge upon your basic moral standing.

Conceptually speaking, there are many different ways in which equality of moral worth can be affirmed. One might say, for instance, that we are equal in the eyes of God; one might even drive home the sheer creatureliness of our existence to question invidious distinctions, such as Kabir does, with his characteristic forthrightness, in this doha: 'It's all one skin and bone, one piss and shit, one blood one meat. From one drop, a universe. Who's a Brahmin? Who's a Shudra?' Older texts like the Mahabharata, while legitimizing caste, also express serious doubt about the institution. Within Indian history, religious traditions and traditions of dissent, these modes have always been available; but they did not often issue in effective and enduring demands for ordering the texture of social relationships. It is not indeed an impossibility to assert both that we are equal in the eyes of God and that a hierarchical social organization such as caste is defensible; indeed the theoretical radicalism of so many claims to equality in the past was compromised by their practical conservatism. It can be granted that Indian history provides at least some conceptual resources for affirming equality. But the introduction of democracy is radical. Democracy is a way of affirming human dignity by granting individuals civic standing.

In a democracy, the desire for having one's moral worth affirmed, for emptying social space of humiliation, is given open social legitimation and expression.

But, paradoxically, the struggles to affirm one's moral worth do not necessarily take the form of a demand for justice. Rather that struggle can express itself as much through a competitive debasement of others as it can in a demand for reciprocity and mutual recognition. If Rousseau's diagnosis is plausible, the desire for having one's worth acknowledged can express itself in all kinds of debased forms, some that require debasing others. Indeed, the paradox is that while individuals and groups can be acutely conscious of society's indifference towards them, they can, in turn, be acutely indifferent towards others. Undeniably, you would almost experience this to be the case in highly inegalitarian societies. The only meaning empowerment has in such a society is power *over* others, some claim of power or privilege or access that sets *you* apart, rather than a sense of empowerment that all can share. The irony is that the more unequal the background institutions and practices of society, the more likely it is that politics will be a struggle to displace the holders of power rather than an ambition to bring about social transformation. The struggle to move ahead will not be a common one for justice—for little commonality exists—but a competitive quest for power. A society that is adept at humiliating its members is more likely to make them adept at humiliating others than teach them about justice.

This perhaps explains one of the paradoxes at the heart of Indian politics. There are few other democracies where the universalist language of injustice, rights, even constitutionalism is so profusely used and has become part of so many political mobilizations. But this is a stratagem for particular individuals or groups to gain access to power, not an acknowledgement of the due claims of all. Discourses of law, constitutionalism, rights, justice, obligations, do not signify that a particular set of values are being taken as authoritative and these set genuine moral constraints for individuals. Rather, they are the languages in which particular grievances are expressed or interests advanced without the least acknowledgement of reciprocal or parallel interests and grievances of others. A sense of justice towards someone presupposes a sense of reciprocity, it presupposes that you acknowledge others. The more the social distance, the less likely that such reciprocity obtains. It is quite possible for a democracy to experience great clamour for recognition by particular individuals and groups without these resulting in diffusion of norms of justice. This follows the general pattern of the ways in which Indian society has been democratized. Democracy in India has advanced through competitive negotiations between groups, each competing for their interests, rather than the diffusion of democratic norms. It is, in some senses, a contingent outcome of social conflicts, not necessarily a deep-seated norm.

Discourses on equality will be culturally specific, because in part these will have to confront the terms and reasons that classes of people have for feeling humiliated. 'The equality of what' question has to be answered in terms of some understanding of the kinds of inequalities that people find injurious to their self-respect. This is not to say that only those inequalities that are seen as such are the only ones that need redressal. That is an open question. But the powerful mobilizing impulses come from a sense that an injury to self-respect needs redressal. This sense can sometimes be genuine. In the case of some groups, Hindu nationalism for instance, it can be a product of ideological displacement and mystification, where we compensate for potentially losing our status, both in relation to other groups in society and often in relation to our standing to the wider world, by presenting ourselves as victims under threat. But it is no accident that arguably all the potent mobilizations that independent India has seen, in some respects, involve an appeal to self-respect. Most of our politics has been a politics of recognition. Appeals to self-respect stand in a complicated relation to material determinants and it would be misunderstanding their potency to simply make them instrumental to class interests. If politics in independent India has demonstrated anything, it is this: that a sense of injury that galvanizes people into political action can be politically created, and not just materially determined. 'Politically created' should not be taken to mean simply what it means in common parlance—serving the interests of politicians. It is rather the complicated process by which we represent our place in the world to ourselves, through ideologies, myth, rituals, rites and collective enactments of all kinds. It is one of the striking features of politics in India that so many of its most significant political energies have come from movements that, in some respect, engage in what we might call a politics of self-esteem. Movements otherwise as diverse as the Dravidian movement, the Shiv Sena, the Bahujan Samaj Party (BSP), or even for that matter the Bharatiya Janata Party (BJP), have in some ways tapped into this politics. Although these movements have a distinctive social base, are animated by different political ends, and are shaped by the particular regional histories from where they emerged and are sustained by different incentive structures, each also powerfully appeals to the language of self-esteem. Each of these is, amongst other things, an assertion of an identity; each thrives upon the creation of a discourse where there is some 'other', imagined or real, who is the cause of oppression or threatening in some other way. The fact that so much of our politics is about self-esteem is a testament that somewhere, and in complicated ways, this society mutilates the self-respect, the sense of moral worth of individuals enough to make them attracted to such a politics. The dispossessed may engage in it because their structural position warrants it; the privileged may be susceptible because of gnawing anxiety and uncertainty about their status in a rapidly changing world. This is also why so much of our politics is less oriented towards collectively solving practical problems, but is governed by the allure of asserting one's own will. Politics in India is a peculiar way of feeling assertive and alive—that gives politics its appeal and its edge.

India's experience with democracy is anomalous in one significant sense. India was one of the few societies where a political revolution preceded a social one. When Tocqueville discussed the great contrast between two ways of conceiving the relationship between social and political equality, he had this contrast in mind. On the one hand there was America that, because of the peculiar absence of feudalism, inherited social equality of sorts. In France, on the other, social equality, although many centuries in the making and shaped fundamentally by Christianity, was ultimately brought about through social revolution, through a violent overthrow of the aristocracy. In India, the nationalist movements and the social reform that sometimes accompanied it, and sometimes was demanded in opposition to it, prepared some of the ideological ground for equality, in that it at least, to a certain extent, delegitimized the most egregious forms of oppression that characterized the Hindu society. But despite this delegitimization, the structure of what we might call India's social ancien régime, survived into democracy relatively intact. That whole ensemble of different rights, privileges that stratified Indian society and produced some of the vilest forms of social distinctions known, was carried over into the democratic framework. The contradiction, between proclaimed political equality on the one hand, and deep social and economic equality on the other, was too obvious to go unnoticed. But this feature, in part, constituted the uniqueness of the Indian experiment. Rather than political democracy following at least a social transformation of sorts, ultimately it was going to be the instrument of this transformation.

Just to take one example: think of how peculiar India's experience of land reform has been. In most postcolonial societies, agrarian relations, if they were transformed at all, were transformed either through radical revolutions, that literally decimated the upper classes, or by forms of colonialism, for example, the

Japanese in Korea, that completely dismantled the landed classes decisively. India's colonial powers, for all their penetration into the society, were, in this sense, relatively conservative, highly unlikely to radically reconstitute agrarian relations once their power had been established. India is one of the few countries that attempted land reform through democratic means. Although its success was limited and uneven, that should not detract from the enormity and anomalousness of what was being attempted. Right from the start, therefore, the project of social transformation was hostage to negotiations between different groups mobilizing and jostling for power in a setting of competitive politics. This undoubtedly gave the privileged certain advantages. Land reforms, although they managed to abolish zamindari, were limited for a number of reasons, in part because dominant interests managed to circumvent it. Tocqueville's prophecy that in democracies, perhaps even in indigent ones, the poor will rarely vote to dispossess the rich has also some bearing on this story. But it is also an instance of the way in which the dismantling of India's ancien régime, in the context of democratic politics, would necessarily be ameliorative rather than radical. Paradoxically, it might turn out that democratic regimes are probably less successful in instituting social equality than authoritarian ones. The price of democracy is the absence of revolution. But suggesting that India might have come out better had it experienced a violent revolution, or a state bent on recreating social relations from scratch, is to perhaps engage too much in the condescension of posterity. Though it did turn out, retrospectively, that democracy is no quick fix for the challenge of inequality.

Social equality as an ideal has been slow to impress itself upon modern Indian politics. This is, in some cases, a banal truism. Many of those social practices and institutions, through which the subordination, deprivation and often humiliation of large numbers of Indian citizens is daily legitimized and re-enacted, remain in place.

One simple explanation for the greater *ideological* acceptance of equality at the time of independence would be that it did not cost much. When claims about equality began to proliferate from the nineteenth century onwards, these largely remained claims. They were, for the most part, rhetorical stratagems, but most of the privileged that articulated them did not seriously expect them to immediately issue in a reordering of social relations that jeopardized their positions of privilege. Just as the Constitution was a radical idea, without itself containing guarantees that the social transformation it promised would come about, so are most claims to equality. Indeed, programmes of social reform undertaken in the name of equality can reposition old elites in new positions of power. So the cynical interpretation would go: equality, in whatever terms it was embraced, was not thought to constitute any real risk to privilege. Indeed, it sometimes offset the risk posed to privilege by not embracing equality. Acceding to claims of equality allowed strategic management of social protest, but the limits to which it was practised were defined by the imperatives of that strategic incorporation. Appeals to equality were seldom a means to reconstitute social relations; they were, at best, a move within existing relations of power.

Caste and Politics:
Anti-Caste or Anti-Upper-Caste?

One of the most significant axes around which the politics of equality is conducted is caste. The origins and significance of caste as an institution are complicated, and the reasons for its enduring power still a matter of contention. But there is no doubt that by the nineteenth century, when the process of social reform of Indian society began in earnest, caste was one of the most egregiously hierarchical systems of rank ordering the entitlements, privileges and even the sense of being of particular groups that human history has known, inflicting unspeakable degradation upon those who were unfortunate enough to be at the lower ends of the hierarchy, such as the untouchables. During the nineteenth century, there were various apologetics on behalf of the caste system, but gradually a consensus emerged that whatever the rationale for the system, in its present form, with the ways in which it mutilated human beings, it could not be defended. Reform of the caste system became an object of concern for some high-caste Hindus, but more significantly for autonomous lower-caste movements, like Narayana Guru's in Kerala, and Phule's in Maharashtra. Much of the upper-caste effort in reforming caste was, and still remains, motivated by the desire to consolidate Hinduism. The idea was that as the lowest castes became politically conscious, they would dissociate themselves from Hinduism, if it did not reform itself and give the marginalized social spaces to lead lives with dignity and self-respect. All of these movements had the effect of changing the culture of legitimation beyond recognition. By the time Independence came, there were few apologists for the caste system left. Untouchability was abolished, and many professed to discouraging the perpetuation of caste, even though in practice the system had not been as substantially dented as many reformers had hoped.

But it was not just the reality of caste that remained disturbing. The modalities of social reform were themselves an object of concern. Many untouchables, especially, found an upper-caste concern with their plight patronizing because it did little to empower them. Moreover, the agency of reform, and the terms on which it was going to be conducted, were still going to be defined by upper-caste noblesse oblige, not the agency of the oppressed themselves. Even Gandhi, for all his extraordinary personal commitment, and mastery of the dramatic gestures that could symbolically make a dent into any ideology like no one else could, increasingly began to be tainted with this suspicion. Matters had already come to a head in the Ambedkar–Gandhi dispute over separate electorates that came to symbolize the aporias of caste reform.

Both had creditable motives. Gandhi thought that separate electorates would divide Hinduism deeply and forever. Such a division would polarize society and impede the creation of common political projects and a sense of mutuality. Separate electorates could also be potentially self-defeating if it gave upper castes a reason to entrench their positions on reform. Gandhi, above all, wanted upper castes to feel guilty and atone for the egregious domination and privileges they enjoyed. Ambedkar, on the other hand, thought that invoking common purposes or the unity of Hindu society was simply to disguise the deep sense of oppression and fissure that existed within the society. If Gandhi thought that emphasizing division would give rise to violence, Ambedkar powerfully argued that this would be probably no worse than the violence that already characterized Hindu society, and in any case violence would be a result of assertion of power by the upper castes. Upper-caste guilt was not good enough and was unlikely to lead to an enduring change. What was required was the creation of conditions and social spaces where the untouchables and lower castes could feel empowered and act with a sense of agency. The result was a compromise which, although it disallowed separate electorates, legitimized the principle that greater political representation, through reserved seats, was not only a measure of the state's commitment to be more representative, it was also the means through which social empowerment would be brought about. Access to jobs for Dalits and later Other Backward Castes (OBCs), via the state and educational institutions, became a central feature of the Indian programme of ameliorative reform. Like most state policies, reservations for Scheduled Castes were implemented largely in the breach, especially in Class I and Class II forms of employment, until political mobilization forced the state to take its own provisions seriously.

The emphasis on an effective sense of agency, rather than simply the removal of inequity was thus inscribed into the aspirations of lower-caste politics from very early on. But the perception of being disempowered tends to be mediated through a collective identity of some sort. It is by virtue of being a member of a particular group, or a particular jati, that discrimination, subordination and outright oppression are experienced. Therefore, the discourse of equality in Indian democracy often seeks to achieve equality between groups. It aims not at liberating individuals from groups, or even necessarily eroding the structural logic of the system that makes group rankings possible in the first place. Arguably, in that sense, the forms of caste politics we are witnessing have some continuities with caste politics in older periods of Indian history. There have been many modes of protest against caste, though none have enduringly dismantled its central logic. It is debatable whether individual renouncers had caste, but it certainly was a mode of protest available. Withdrawal and self-organization of small groups, as happened with some bhakti and tantric cults, was also an option occasionally exercised. Ideologies like Buddhism and Jainism at least unsettled legitimations of caste; though in the end they proved to be more anti-brahminical than anti-caste.

Castes have often transformed their position by aspiring to upward mobility, either through Sanskritization, or, what for want of a better word might be described as Kshatriyaization, the attempts of castes to gain access to state power. In this sense, as many recent writers on caste have suggested, politics was as central to the constitution, status and identities of particular castes as ritual. For example, as Susan Bayly has argued, the cluster of castes we have now come to designate as being Rajput were not constituted through ritual meaning but by their entitlements to be enrolled in privileged military service within the Mughal kingdom. These changes, again, are at best changes in the positional status of particular castes, not a transformation of caste itself. But what is significant historically, in instances of caste mobility, is this: through access to state power, a hitherto lower caste can displace other castes and acquire prominence. In part, the prospects for such upward mobility depend upon opportunities for the same. The more consolidated political rule is, the more secure the social foundations of any kingdom, the less likely it is that new groups will emerge to claim power. Perhaps this is a little speculation here, but I suspect that periods immediately after the collapse of great empires such as the Mughal or Vijayanagar empires, or areas where the hold of those empires is tenuous, provide the greatest opportunities for such mobility. In a sense, a period of consolidated empires, such as the British Empire, dampens the opportunity for caste competition for political power to emerge. While it is patently mystifying to suggest that caste was invented under colonialism, it is more plausible to claim that the British Empire consolidated a nexus of particular castes with political power: the Brahmin–Company Raj, as it is sometimes dubbed.

In a way, Independence once again reopened the possibilities for caste competition. The very imperatives of mobilization under universal suffrage made all castes potential candidates for the same. While previously in Indian history there were periods of confined competition between different groups for access to political power, democracy opened and generalized this competition. It was certainly not an overdetermined outcome that caste would be the principal axis of mobilization, nor should the existence of caste competition lead one to assume that there is a strict correlation between castes and voting preferences. But because caste mobilization can appeal to a politics of self-respect, because a sense of shared identity can help overcome collective action problems, and because socially it is an axis of self-recognition, its salience in politics was inevitable.

But its results varied considerably. In south India, because of the peculiar demographic distribution of the 'higher varnas' and the ability of the lower castes to share a sense of regional identity, their incorporation into the state was relatively more successful. In general, however, two features dominated caste politics. One was the fact that all groups were, in principle, equally competing for power, but which does not mean that they would all treat each other equally. All groups acquired the right to compete, and air their demands, but could be completely indifferent to similar demands from other groups. This is why broad alliances of lower-caste groups have been relatively few and unstable, for instance, the OBCs from the 1950s and 1960s did not last long, and while the Mandal Commission gave OBC groups in north India a new political identity, its cohesion must not be exaggerated. Broad-based lower-caste alliances have had more success, where, as Christophe Jaffrelot has shown, they have 'ethnicized' themselves, that is, mobilized on the basis of a shared regional identity such as Marathas or Dravidians. The second and perhaps more crucial point is this: as the competition for power becomes keener, and as the upper castes are gradually displaced from political power, the intensity of competition amongst lower-caste groups is likely to increase. In the case of OBCs and Dalits in UP, many of their economic interests clearly diverge, but there will also be an intense competition amongst castes within each of these broad categories. This is for the following reason: *To put it provocatively, we have arguably never had an anti-caste politics. What we have witnessed in the decades since Independence is anti-upper-caste politics.* The main aim is to muster as much clout as you can to displace the groups that currently hold power. It is the virtue of our democracy that this has become an open-ended game; it is our limitation that we assume that displacing upper or currently dominant castes is the same thing as social transformation.

In some ways, the trajectory of caste mobilizations in north India has turned out to be one of the huge disappointments of the last decade. Caste politics was seen by many as one of the defining narratives of Indian politics in two senses. In a mundane sense, caste is often seen as a determinant predictor of political behaviour and allegiances. To what extent it is, is debatable. But in a deeper sense, the narrative of caste-based politics was seen as profoundly progressive and emancipatory. This would be the ideological axis that would stop Hindutva in its tracks, that would deliver social justice to the most oppressed of the oppressed, signify a deepening of Indian democracy where the hitherto oppressed took the reins of power in their own hands to shake the society from its inegalitarian stupor. Great hopes were invested in OBCs, Dalits and Adivasis. Not since Marx had reposed his hopes in the proletariat had any other social groups had to carry such burden of being agents of social change. Like Marx's proletariat, these oppressed groups had nothing to lose but their chains; like Marx's proletariat, they were not morally contaminated by occupying positions of power and privilege, and like the proletariat, their suffering would give them a unique consciousness about society's workings that would allow them to progressively transform it.

Certainly, a great deal of churning happened in Indian politics as a result. The social composition of government and politics began to change; orthodox Manuwadis went scurrying for cover, and even the brahminical BJP had to accept Mandal. Laloo and Mayawati became harbingers of the dignity and self-respect of millions. Indian democracy was coming of age. Only sullenly resentful upper-caste folks and their ideological cronies could think otherwise. In urban India, upper castes took to seceding from public institutions; in the countryside, they often resorted to even greater atrocities. Brutal caste violence continued, but even this had a silver lining. It showed that oppression was not going unchallenged and the writ of the Thakurs could not run large without provoking resistance. The age of emancipation was finally at hand. Intellectuals, ever eager to be on the winning side of history, proclaimed the solidarity of the oppressed, gave voice to the voiceless, and reposed their hopes in this great moral churning.

To be sure, there were hiccups on the way. Laloo was in the process of taking Marx's advice to the proletariat seriously: once the oppressed seize the state apparatus, they should dismantle it. Mayawati was trying to ensure that the best way of expressing solidarity with her constituents was by making sure that UP remained where it was in human development. But these infractions were simply part of the process of consciousness raising. An insolent and conflictual polity that weakened the hold upper castes had on political power was, we surmised, better than the insidious torture that India's social system had heaped upon its less privileged. What good had the existing system of protecting privileges ever done for the downtrodden? Will not a system that had perfected the art of humiliation produce a competitive and violent politics in turn, bereft of any reciprocity? There was much truth in this description. It drew its pathos from the fact that all the promises hitherto made to dismantle the most insidious forms of human inequality any society had ever devised had failed. Gandhism was no more than a patronizing gesture, Nehruvianism with its great hopes in the emancipatory power of the state was floundering, and the great liberal project of treating individuals as individuals was simply rendering oppression invisible. A major shake-up was required as a prelude to social justice. A second great democratic revolution.

If anyone had faith in the unambiguously emancipatory trajectory of this revolution, its actual unfolding came as a shock. Mayawati's continual cosying up to the BJP, whatever the compulsions of politics, laid to rest any illusions that north India's first great Dalit-based party would herald a new dawn in the annals of politics. The participation of Adivasis in violence against Muslims in Gujarat destroyed any hope that shared vulnerabilities would produce shared solidarities. Mandal is no longer the enduring antidote to Mandir that we hoped it would be. The so-called anti-caste crusades in north India, turn out, on inspection, to have been nothing other than anti-upper-caste stratagems, which is not quite the same thing. In keeping with India's tradition of involuted pluralism, the deeper, more intractable and violent fault lines are everywhere evident between Dalits and OBCs and amongst the Dalits themselves. The term 'upper-caste oppression' is still used profusely, but its referents have, in some instances, changed simply to refer to any new group that acquires power. Outside of intellectual circles, which always have an investment in hope, nobody in politics seems to believe in shared solidarities of the oppressed. Caste solidarity went the way of class solidarity.

Of course, the inequalities and oppressions that occasioned the need for a struggle for social justice continue unabated in a myriad forms. It would be important not to let the cynicism induced by the sordid and corrupt forms that caste politics have taken to obscure the real suffering this social system so diligently reproduces and so casually tolerates. But one thing is clear. These will require, as the recent Bhopal declaration acknowledges, an even more imaginative response than simply having faith in the power of the oppressed to eliminate the sources of oppression once they are given the reins of power. No social group, as a group is, can be a unique and unequivocal bearer of an emancipatory aspiration. The oppressed in our system ought to command our moral attention, because that is the demand for justice. But often the trust we repose in those who claim to have arisen from the mantle of oppression is misplaced. It is a reflection more of our desire to avoid misanthropy than of actual political realities. To avoid hating the world, we hope that its victims will, at least, carry forward the cause of justice. But to idealize every political disposition that seeks to legitimize itself in the moral aura of victimhood is a potentially dangerous illusion. Indeed, if the general patterns of politics are any guide, particularistic aspirations, rather than claims for justice, will mark almost all political movements in India. That by itself does not make them illegitimate, but there is also no reason to impute more transformative hopes to them than reality warrants. And contrary to fears that caste politics would lead to undue divisions, it turns out that what those who engage in caste politics share is far more important than what divides them: a taste for politics. Caste politics is the triumph of politics over caste.

That caste politics in the last two decades has largely confined itself to the ambition of gaining access to power rather than any substantial agenda of social transformation is patently clear and not altogether surprising. The question is what does this portend for a genuinely egalitarian society? On one line of thought, the claim that parties such as the BSP and the Rashtriya Janata Dal (RJD) are not harbingers of social change is profoundly misleading. The fact that they have opened up political spaces, even if they have enacted and legitimized their own brand of violence, is itself a transformative moment. At the very least, it does not leave their Dalit constituents at the mercy of a state whose daily interaction with them was often no better than the violent dominant castes that the state was supposed to protect them from. Second, in so far as access to power is itself a necessary, if not a sufficient, condition for a wider transformation of Indian society, caste mobilizations that give them access are a step forward. Third, it is important to understand why caste acquired such a salience in politics in the first place. It was in part due to the fact that caste was an axis of domination and subordination in Indian society; it was in part due to the fact that the search for social coalitions inevitably involves appeals to group identities, and in part due to the fact that the state itself, by sanctioning categories of caste, provided the incentives to mobilize. But fundamentally, caste emerged as a salient political category not because it is simply a regressive primordial identity that benighted voters were condemned to because they are incapable of thinking beyond a narrow circle of loyalties. It is rather because there were few other competing ideologies that allowed people to make sense of their social circumstances in the way caste did. Perhaps mobilizations should have taken place on a more social democratic basis; perhaps these should have coalesced around more universalistic demands for health, education, welfare and a partial reordering of property rights. But is there anything in Indian historical experience that would convince anyone that the state can be anything other than selective in targeting benefits, and it targets them based on which groups have access to power? Since the collective costs of action for mobilizing caste groups (as opposed to forming broad-based coalitions) is relatively more manageable, it was a *rational* choice around which to mobilize. Caste mobilization is not an indictment of those who mobilize along those lines; it is an indictment of the entire experience of Indian politics, which leaves caste as amongst the salient vocabularies within which to understand the terms of oppression and deprivation. There is a lot of self-serving horror at the use of caste vocabularies in politics. This horror is self-serving because it comes with a kind of easy moralism that is often an obstacle to social self-knowledge. The fact that caste has proved to be so sticky and acquired new salience in politics is seen as a kind of moral mistake, a self-serving departure from the happy aspirations of our liberal constitutionalism to simply a ruse to gain access to power. In part, this moralism against the use of caste in politics is disingenuous because it pretends to be ignorant about the forms that oppression took in Indian society, and dwells in the comfortable illusion that just because there was a constitutional settlement, all forms of caste oppression disappeared. In part, it is indigenous because it does not ask questions about how to create social spaces where caste bonds are loosened. Can they be loosened if there is little social or spatial mobility? Can this mobility come about in the absence of opportunity? Marriage is one of the principal means by which caste ties are reproduced across generations. There is something to the supposition that until inter-caste marriage becomes the norm, rather than the exception, caste will have a social salience that cannot but have political ramifications. But how do you create a society where inter-caste marriages are the norm? Certainly, they have to be made ideologically acceptable, in part by making the idea that individuals, men and women, should exercise their choices acceptable. But more than that, other social spaces have to be created where there is a sense in which individuals can meaningfully exercise choice, spaces where men and women mix. Other than a few urban pockets, these spaces still do not exist. It is somewhat odd to wish away reality of caste when society is not willing to invest in creating opportunities that decrease its importance. There is some evidence from urban India, where there are opportunities and social spaces, that it is already on the decline.

If worrying about the salience of caste in politics without redressing the underlying causes is not constructive, and is often disingenuous, worrying about what political leaders will do, once empowered through an idiom of caste, is. Arguably, the left in India, in its zeal to indict existing inequalities, has mostly turned a blind eye to the limitations and human costs that particular form of caste mobilizations in states such as UP and Bihar have imposed on their constituents. Access to state power was, in Indian conditions, necessary for bringing about social transformation: there is good evidence that representation not only enhances the self-respect of citizens (there is a sense in which they can begin to call the state their own), it also provides many with protection and helps channel at least the benefits of patronage. But there are inherent limitations to this politics. First, by its very nature it does not have a broad transformative agenda, it is a politics of positional change not structural reform. The second limitation is more contingent. The norms of governance that the leadership of these movements has instituted in north India at least have seriously undermined the ability of the state to be an instrument of social change. I say this is a contingent limitation because there is no necessary reason why the rise of leaders like Mayawati and Laloo Yadav should have enhanced and exacerbated the weaknesses and failures of their respective states. It will not do anyone, especially Dalits, any good, if the state they gain access to becomes unviable and dysfunctional because of the way in which their political leadership destroys it for short-term advantage rather than use it for long-term and sustainable transformation. And finally, there are inherent limits to what the state can achieve by way of creating new opportunity for Dalits and other marginalized groups. Or rather, if the state wants to, it will have to do so through means other than simply giving access to the state's resources.

The truth is this. Unless the newly mobilized Dalit castes can be given access to the gains of the market economy, their prospects for social advancement remain dim. The gains of the market economy can be legitimized only to the extent that Dalits are part of these gains; and they can, in the long run, socially and economically empower themselves only if they acquire the capacities to navigate a market economy successfully. The state has limited resources, its capacities for expansion are at breaking point, and most wealth in society will be generated outside the state. Political power can give Dalits access to state resources that ensures that the latter is not complicit in reproducing social inequity. Access to state jobs and institutions of higher education through affirmative action can be helpful to the extent that it can create a small middle class and challenge the culture of governance that has subordinated Dalits. But beyond that there are limits to what access to state power alone will achieve. As many critics, even some sympathetic to the Dalit cause, have pointed out that the state's resources allocated for affirmative action go to a very small section of the dispossessed. And Dalit groups which gain whatever limited access to power they have acquired are often keener on preserving the privileges of their sub-caste vis-à-vis others than in advancing the general welfare. State power will not by itself enhance Dalit representation in all those walks of life that will be at the cutting edge of the new Indian economy. Historically, the state has been a source of a resource that is often the key to social mobility and economic advancement: education. However, under present circumstances, the Indian state's ability to impart the kind of education that will be the key to economic advancement remains limited. It is now a cliché to say that the modern economy is a knowledge-based economy. It is implausible to suppose that state-run institutions of higher education will in any way be able to produce the kind of knowledge that a modern economy requires. Most of the Indian middle class recognizes this. De facto, they seek access to private institutions or institutions abroad to equip them with the skills required to make headway. The simple fact is that those who are limited to access to state institutions are often condemned to mediocrity.

The imperative of giving Dalits access to the market economy will, in due course, result in a new kind of Dalit politics. This will, in part, be because in a market their prospects for advancement will depend on marketable skills, not on access to state power. This will hopefully reorient the energies of Dalit politics towards the creations of such skills. Whether it will take this direction, and what role the state can play in it, we will discuss in the next section.

The New Culture of Inequality

Caste is not the only area where the insidiousness of inequality impresses itself with an unrelenting force. It not only inflicts injuries upon agents, but also gives the politics that results a competitive edge. There are other areas as well; most powerfully, gender. But I would like to suggest that the subtle psychological ramifications of inequality and humiliation inflect social life in India in the most unexpected places. Tocqueville very perceptively argued that the onset of equality as a social condition could, in some sense, be best gauged by the relations between master and servants in any given society. The onset of democracy will not prevent the existence of these classes; in some senses, there will always be social superiors and social subordinates. The difference between masters and servants in traditional aristocratic societies and democratic societies is that in traditional societies, this relationship has caste-like characteristics. You are a subordinate not simply because you are under a contract to carry out particular tasks; your identity as a servant permeates the whole of your social being and the scope of social possibility. If you are a servant, you cannot sit with the master or in his presence, you cannot inhabit the same social spaces, you may not speak unless spoken to; even in urban settings, there is an ensemble of practices that makes the distance between human beings match the distance between species. Even outside the confines of your workplace, the fact that you are a servant remains an indelible social fact. In democracies, by contrast, Tocqueville's supposition goes, servants will be more like contract labour. They will perform certain tasks, but outside the confines of those tasks, their social identity is not determined by their status as servants. In short, all the restrictions that sustain a profound social distance between master and servant will gradually disappear. There will be a social space in which the servant will be able to assert: 'I am a human being and outside the confines of the particular relationship we have contracted into, I can, in principle, enjoy the same rights as you.' The simple idea is that the terms of inequality will be defined by the particular contractual relationships one enters into. 'I am your servant, your employee, your helper, but your powers and your social standing over me remain confined to the spheres in which I contractually am your subordinate. And my subordinate status in this sphere does not pervade the whole of my social being.'

In India, inequality takes a peculiar form. Take the master–servant relationship in its literal sense. It is probably in some senses true that such relationships, at least in urban India, have undergone some transformation. They are more contractual, there is little expectation that a servant will be a permanent, if often invisible, member of a household, and at least in principle, servants can harbour aspirations to social mobility. This would be a trend that all societies experience. But the peculiarity of the Indian experience consists in this. While the master–servant relations have become more contingent and less of a condition in perpetuity, they still come with a baggage of social practices that give them more caste-like characteristics than their contractual arrangement would suggest. Servants are still routinely targets of reinvented pollution–purity taboos: they may not sit on the same chairs as their masters, if they are allowed to sit at all; their lives are the object of many subtle and unsubtle interdictions that have nothing to do with the task allotted to them. In short, despite the arrangement being more contractual, a sense of servitude is made to pervade their whole social being and social identity. The eradication of caste-based or religiously based taboos has not meant that other marks of cultural subordination that have caste-like characteristics have not been reinvented under democratic conditions.

The net result is that the condition that Tocqueville foresaw as happening under democracies has not come about. As he had put it, 'Within the terms of the contract, one is servant and the other master; beyond that, they are two citizens and two men.' This phenomenon is of obvious importance to India's democratic experience for the following reason. Not only is it a vivid exemplification that human equality in the most basic sense does not have much of an impress on Indian social mores, it is also a grim reminder that it may not do so even in urban settings which one might have expected to be free of at least classical caste-like taboos. And it is also a reminder that the sense in which inequality bears down upon citizens goes far beyond the inequalities that attend to straightforward class distinctions. For most individuals, there is no 'beyond' the terms of the contract where their claims to equality can be meaningfully experienced.

But the most important reason to address the master-servant distinction is that far from being superseded, this distinction, in some ways, pervades most social relations in India. Take for instance our public institutions, where these very distinctions are inscribed into the Class I–IV structure that pervades them. And as most of us have commonly experienced, the inequality is not confined simply to the sphere within which it is legitimized but inflects the entire gamut of social relationships as well. The Tocquevillian thought that 'outside the terms of my official employment I am not a peon' is very hard to believe with a degree of conviction, and will rapidly vanish the minute you encounter your boss, even outside the confines of office. To put it crudely, your sahib remains a sahib, whether in office or not. The standard narrative of 'status' to 'contract' does not posit the diminution of inequality; what it suggests is that it would be possible for individuals to have a standing independent of the particular inequalities they were placed in position of by virtue of class, talent or whatever. India has managed to reproduce so many of the caste-like behavioural distinctions within the framework of contractual relationships.

What democracy has done is that it has brought into the open and qualitatively enhanced the force of a phenomenon that probably always existed. A sense of upward contempt is now more often available to those who, in traditional terms, were defined as being of lower rank. It now accompanies the usual contempt that the privileged express. Indeed, ironically, the sense that many privileged express that 'master–servant' relations are more conflictual, or that the relations between different ranks of employees are more sullen, may exemplify this. What Indian democracy has done is that it has produced a new form of reciprocity: a reciprocity of contempt.

But more significantly, I want to suggest somewhat provocatively that the master–servant relationship, rather than being the superseded, is the paradigm exemplar of most social relations in India. The one thing that strikes any observer with overwhelming force is the quality of human relationship even in so-called professional institutions: universities, corporations, public sector enterprises and so forth. One gets the impression the professional hierarchies that are legitimately internal to the workings of these organizations have immense social ramifications beyond simply the professional. Anecdotally, the deference given to superiors in most organizations takes forms far beyond those mandated by the hierarchy of professional roles. The most public and vivid instance of this is of course the feigned but abject servility towards those in power, or in some senses superior to you.

This fact has subtle implications for the texture of social relationships in Indian society, which in turn has profound ramifications for democracy. First, it makes social competition within organizations more intense; there is a lot more at stake in losing out than simply lower income or something straightforward. It is rather that a whole web of acknowledgements and courtesies, a vast panoply of privileges and entitlements accrue to positions of power that have nothing to do with the professional or publicly defined role. Second, because inequality is a marker not just of distinction in a particular area or along one particular dimension, say professional accomplishment, or wealth, or talent or whatever, but comes to define your broad status, the social meaning of your role comes to overwhelm its distinctive characteristics.

There is a good deal of consternation over the fact that 'merit' becomes an anathema under democratic pressure. The argument is made that it is the democratic impulse to level down, to seek equality as such, that crowds out any consideration of merit that is seen as a deviation from democratic norms or a threat to equality. In their different ways, Sudipta Kaviraj and

Andre Beteille have expressed worries on this score. Or the argument is made that the requirements of giving socially marginalized groups access to positions of power and privilege through affirmative action have made merit an issue of secondary concern. While there is something to be said for both these tendencies in Indian democracy, the real issue is somewhat different. What supersedes considerations of merit is the fear that any distinction or achievement is simply a way of dominating others. Achievement might make you not just better in that sphere, it might make you an altogether different species. Again, as Rousseau so presciently pointed out, in deeply inegalitarian societies there will be little honest appraisal of merit or genuine achievement, because most find it difficult to believe that others' achievement can be anything other than another means of dominating them. There is an excessive focus on the status achievement might bring rather than the achievement itself, which explains why we are so keen to pull down real merit, and why so much of our organizational politics is focused on gaining power rather than achieving something. The lurking fear that achievement or advancement might give someone the power to negate you, or debase you, detracts from a focus on excellence in its own right.

I want to venture the supposition that the peculiar characteristics that accompany competition for status often impede effective collective action. In a sociological sense, this is true: states where there is a greater social distance and inequality between citizens often find collective action in politics more difficult. Many observers of different institutions have often noted the disquieting tendency with which professional disagreements are quickly converted into personal slights. Losing an argument is seen as a loss in status. This makes envy take a peculiarly self-destructive form. Envy, a sentiment characteristic of many different societies, can take different forms. It can mean that I wish for what you have, but not necessarily that I wish it at your expense. Or it can be that I feel resentful not simply because I don't possess something, but because *you* do. In the former case, envy can be productive, specific and disinterested at the same time. Productive because it can be a spur to action; specific because it is occasioned by a particular desire; and disinterested because it doesn't grudge what others have, it only wishes that one had that as well. Any generalizations in this area are hazardous and run the risk of essentialism. Such envy is an altogether democratic sentiment and, as Tocqueville argued, entirely to be expected. But such envy does not necessarily have to take the form of a zero-sum game; it does not have to involve the thought that my well-being depends upon your doing less well. But expressions of envy in the context of social relations in India often take a different form.

It takes the form of a generalized resentment against success; in organizational relationships, it leads to a disposition where there is more interest in preventing others from getting something than there is in making yourself worthy of that achievement. In part, envy takes this form because not having something involves a greater risk of status deprivation. To not have an official position, for instance, or to not have wealth, is not merely an absence of that good. It is the absence of a recognition altogether. To summarize the structure of the argument, envy is a product of inegalitarian social relations, where the consequences of inequality in a particular sphere is a denial of social standing altogether. Distinctions along particular dimensions will rapidly translate into social distinctions as such: you have to stand for the other person, call them sir, and see them get access to places where their particular position should not matter. In short, you will be subordinated as such. All societies have inequalities along particular dimensions and all societies have their own forms of social distance between the different classes. But there are few societies where inequality leads to social distancing of the most humiliating kind in as pronounced a way as India, almost a kind of social death.

It is difficult to imagine that societies, which are characterized by such enormous social distance across the whole sphere of its collective institutions, can be very effective at collective action. Stephen Rosen has even made a powerful argument to the effect that some of the weaknesses of the Indian military are due to the fact that it reproduces many forms of social distancing that the civilian society practices. Military hierarchy is not just a military hierarchy; it defines a wider range of social privileges and superior attitudes as well. The same is true of most other institutions. I once met a Japanese businessman with considerable interests in India. I was asking him the usual boring questions of what it was like to do business in India, why it was not a more attractive destination for investment, why the Indian economy was not doing better and so on. The answer he gave was surprising. Government controls, bad labour laws, poor infrastructure were all an impediment to the growth, as we all know. But he suggested that in the final analysis, the Achilles heel of Indian industry was going to be the quality of human relationships. He did not mean just the obvious fact that managers and labour are probably more socially distant. That they are, everywhere. It is that this social distance is of unfathomable depth. But more surprisingly, he argued, it was the quality of relations within the managerial hierarchy, where he had the distinct impression that if you scratch the top, you will find more energies devoted to undercutting each other, than to thinking collectively and over the long run. The acuteness of status competition overrides the professional imperatives of strategic thinking. There can be little unity of purpose without underlying social reciprocity. Even in an urban setting, this exemplifies something that most research on demand for the provision of health and education has shown, that deep social inequalities inhibit collective action and the emergence of common purposes.

What I have been trying to suggest is that the psychic distortions and compromises produced by living in a society whose members do not acknowledge each other as equals in some basic sense, where the social basis for self-respect is generally wanting, will affect even the sentiments and dispositions of those most privileged in it, and often their social interactions as well. The point of dwelling on all this is twofold: first, I have spoken of the moral costs of social inequality in settings that might seem immune to them. I certainly don't want to make the ridiculous suggestion that the deprivations produced by inequality in these settings are nearly as crushing as those experienced by most overwhelmingly oppressed sections of society. Rather, it is to suggest that there is something about the practice of social inequality that afflicts even the most modern sectors of Indian society. 'Caste discrimination' is not simply happening over there in rural India, a sign of our superstitious and feudal inheritance, with their taboos of purity and pollution, fixed notions of hierarchy and so on. It is rather that the master–servant paradigm, even when underwritten by the fiction of contract, and independent of any religious significance, reproduces an insidious form of social distancing. If caste impeded the recognition of equality in a basic sense— comprising equality of human beings, our newly invented forms of contractual inequalities—because they are located in a context where the moral worth of most people, as experienced in their daily interactions, is seldom secure—are doing the same thing. And shades of that social distancing inflect social relations even within those at the top of the hierarchy. Think of the ramifications of forms of social distance that slight people, for vast areas of our collective existence. The one thing we know is that communities, states and social organizations with less social stratification are more effective as collective agents, and many of our failings at collective action come from a sense of social distance.

Take another phenomenon we are preoccupied with: corruption. Corruption is a complex phenomenon, which draws on several different motives and incentives. The seduction of corruption is not simply the desire for money. It is rather the fact that on display an act of corruption is an exercise of power and often of impunity. Impunity, in the sense that corruption is a way of asserting that one is above others, that there is no authority either of persons, or office, to which one is subordinate. Corruption may be seductive, because it gives those who are corrupt a sense of power. In a society which does not often acknowledge the worth and value of individuals, where the visible means of proving one's worth through substantial achievement are open only through a few, corruption is a way of saying that one is somebody. A society without reciprocal forms of mutual recognition is a prime candidate for being a corrupt society because people will compensate for their experience of powerlessness and lack of affirmation of their worth through a competitive exercise of power. Corruption is just one manifestation of that. This will afflict the privileged as well, since their status anxieties will be even greater in such a society than those of the dispossessed.

Or next time just ponder the frequent complaint that Indians lack civic sense—we can gleefully defile public spaces in all sorts of ways. In so far as this is true, it is because in India, public spaces, for most, can never be properly regarded as their own. It is a not a space where most feel they are accorded recognition and standing of any kind; hence there is no reason to care for it.

The burden of the preceding argument has been to show that democracy draws much of its potency from its ability to grant individuals civic standing. But in a society marked at all levels by invidious distinctions of status, politics will often take the form of a competitive quest for dominating others, not a collective enterprise to solve practical problems.

The insidious ways in which social distinctions persist in forms that deny individuals minimum standing and social consideration permanently affect us. The social contradictions also produce a civil war within our souls: a civil war between a desire that we be accorded recognition on the one hand, and, on the other, the sense that this recognition can come only by dominating others. A democracy cannot flourish until it recognizes, as Aurobindo memorably put it, 'every time a society crushes or effaces the individual, it is inflicting a wound on itself and depriving its own life of priceless stimulation and growth'. The subtleties of what dharma means evade most of us. But Yudhisthira's succinct definition in the Mahabharata, that dharma is non-injury (ānṛśaṃsya), is as good an aspiration for democracy to have as any other; it picks out the fundamental fact that a sense of injury, in its widest meaning, can permanently scar us. The practices of popular authorization alone will not ensure that people do not have reason to feel injured. We cannot have a civic life or unity of purpose, because we are not yet equals. Instead of 'United we stand, divided we fall', as nationalists preach, 'equal we stand, unequal we fall' might be a more appropriate explanation for our ills.

Inequality produces a debasing competitive politics, modes of governance that do not acknowledge our moral standing, and most importantly, it produces a social world in which we never quite feel at home.

State and Democracy

If the absence of any sense of reciprocity and mutual acknowledgement between citizens leaves a profound imprint on the character of Indian politics by generating an elusive politics of self-esteem, the workings of the Indian state reveal much about the limits, possibilities and meaning of democracy. The spectral scenes of human misery that still persist in crushing abundance are, in some ways, an indictment of democracy. Despite the improvements of the last decade or so, even a basic recitation of India's human development indices, a casual perusal of their landscape, will bring home the violence built into India's political economy with unnerving force. But the sad truth remains that we mostly pay attention to these facts, if at all, mainly because they are an embarrassment to us, not because we experience them as profoundly unjust. The fact that we are more embarrassed than outraged by these is a sign of the distances that separate us as citizens.

A full assessment of persisting misery despite democracy would require a complex analysis and weighing of different causes: bad policies, the absence of collective action, the weakness of any coherent ideology of reform amongst India's powerful elites, the vice-like grip that vested interests have upon change and so forth. But surely the one agency that will be deeply implicated on this account is the Indian state.

In some ways, all modern societies are creations of the states that house them. The state, for good or for ill, emerged as a decisive form of political organization in the modern world, eclipsing its rivals such as empires, federations, city states, republics. While political thinkers in the Indian tradition have often seen the state as some kind of evil intellectual mistake, because of the enormous violence associated with its formation, the state has proved unprecedented in its capacity to organize collective power, reconstitute social relations, and act as a locus of identity. State formation and consolidation has everywhere extracted horrendous human costs. Despite this, in the modern world it seems that only not having a state is worse than having one. Even in an era when the talk of transcending the nation state is fashionable, it is clear that any organization or supranational entity that seeks to replace it will have to acquire many of the characteristics of a state to be successful.

India inherited a colonial state and kept much of its functioning architecture intact. Much of state practice, despite its massive quantitative expansion, is still heavily governed by legislation passed sometime between 1860 and 1947. In the aftermath of Partition, and in a politics greatly infused with a sense of both territorial insecurity and the lurking fear of internal disorder, the state quickly came to occupy a commanding presence in the Indian political imagination. At the time of Independence, there really existed no institutions that could even remotely rival the state in political legitimacy. The market, in the modern sense of the term, barely existed as a social force. Whatever potential it contained was considered too limited, incapable of bringing real well-being to the masses, and tainted by a moral suspicion of commercial relationships that has been a staple of Indian political discourse: 'Bania civilization', as Nehru contemptuously called it. From the plausible premise that pockets of wealth amidst a sea of poverty are immensely morally problematic, most of India's political spectrum drew the mistaken conclusion that the pursuit of wealth by private individuals and initiative, therefore, had to be delegitimized. In retrospect, it is striking the degree to which a snobbish and moralizing contempt for the market was shared by so many across the political spectrum. It is this attitude, more than its ability to win the technical debate over capital formation, that legitimized the state's control over the economy to an unprecedented degree.

Other institutions fared no better. For all of the nationalist movements, paeans to the innovativeness, adaptability of traditional Indian institutions such as villages, charity organizations, caste associations, there is very little evidence that anyone really thought that they were going to be the medium of social transformation. After all, the ideology of development and the aspirations to justice in the modern sense rendered these institutions suspect—as dens of traditionalism and injustice. Even 'civil society' organizations, of which the Congress itself was an exemplar, were thought to carry very little potential. The state paid its tribute to Gandhism and his emphasis on self-help by nationalizing khadi and making it one more appendage of the state. More than economic concerns, it was a typical statement of the state's confidence in civil society. Even to this day, the non-governmental movement is dogged by the suspicion that the criteria of success is measured by how much of the state's resources and organization it can garner. It was inevitable that all hopes be reposed in the state, and the state would gradually deepen and widen its activities, inserting itself into wider social and economic activity.

And the achievements of the Indian state are, in many ways, remarkable. Its sheer size and power, the thicket of institutions that constitute it, have managed, for the most part to keep India together and to provide a basic framework within which change and renewal, even if only incremental, continue to be possible. It became a palpable source of hope, a locus of organized power that could be made an instrument of transformation. In many sectors of the economy, the state provided the crucial investment; and its role in ameliorating catastrophic horrors like large-scale famine is well documented. Much of its legislation and activity in the social domain has ideologically legitimized social reform, even when it has not been effective. Most importantly, perhaps, the state constituted itself as the locus of material and non-material aspirations alike, politicizing vast areas of society. Although the state has, not surprisingly, been disproportionately captured by dominant groups in society and has had to accommodate itself to them, its redistributive agenda has had mild, if varied success. For all the limitations of land reform, and its limited impact on the well-being of landless labour, zamindari was abolished, and a new class of middle peasants was created, a class whose prominence has widened the social base of Indian democracy.

But the Indian state has been judged to be an unconscionable failure in this sense: for the most part, it has been unable to lift as many out of abject poverty as it promised. This is not the occasion to debate the economic choices the state has made, but there is a sense in which for forty years the state gave us the worst of both worlds. On the one hand, its policies and regulation often dampened growth and the generation of wealth; on the other, the state never developed a full-blown ideological commitment to providing goods such as health and education. The combination of slow growth, only mild possibilities for redistribution, and the absence of any commitment to improve human development indicators, has constantly subjected the state to crises. But the biggest failure of the state has been that it has come to be seen as a symptom of our democratic maladies. The gap between democratic expectations and state action has grown wider. Just think of the contrasting ways in which we now think of the state compared to its official ideology at the time of Independence. It is difficult these days to recreate the sense of idealism and purpose that was associated with the Indian state then. The state had vast reservoirs of legitimacy, and India's elites positioned it as the agency through which democratic aspirations would be realized. The state was going to position itself as an answer to every single failing in society. If society was unequal, the state would provide the space for a discourse of equality; if society was locked into an equilibrium of low productivity, the state would generate economic dynamism by occupying the commanding heights of the economy; if society contained the potential for disorder, the state would be providing order; if society was wrecked by an unbridled pursuit of private interest, the state would be the locus of the common good; where markets did not deliver prosperity, the state would; if society was torn apart with dissension, the state would, through the workings of democracy, be the source of collective will formation.

After nearly five decades, the popular perception of the state is almost the reverse. Rather than rectifying social inequality, it has often reproduced it in its functioning; rather than encouraging productivity, it has in every sense stymied it; rather than provide order, its own odd combination of ineffectiveness and occasional authoritarianism has generated disorder; rather than delivering prosperity, its regulation of the economy has been one of the causes of our poverty; rather than being the locus of democratic aspirations, it constantly subverts them; instead of being the provider of public goods, it has given private interest a free rein and exaggerated its worst tendencies.

Just as there is a danger of over-attributing causal powers to democracy, there is a danger in using as blunt a category as the 'state' to explain all our ills. But there is no doubt that a profound disenchantment with the state is a symptom of democratic discontent. In some ways, a sense of disaffection will be the permanent feature of any modern democracy. No state, even the best intentioned and most well organized, can simultaneously satisfy the diverse expectations imposed upon it, or control the causal processes that might enable it to do so. But the extent to which the state has come to be seen as the subverter of democratic process begs for deeper reflection. This is not the space to have a full-blown discussion on the proper role of the state and the various policy choices the Indian state has made in the past and continues to make. What is of more interest here is the way in which the state comes to be represented, a representation that has now acquired an independent life of its own: whether the state promotes state-led import substitution industrialization or free market integration into the global economy, the discontent is with the *form* of the state itself, not just specific policy choices or ideological convictions.

The almost permanent legitimation crisis that the state faces has several dimensions. Perhaps most alarmingly, the state is unable to uphold the minimum requirements of formal legal rationality attributed to it. The lines between legality and illegality, order and disorder, state and criminality, have come to be increasingly porous. Rather than being an artifice, an impartially superintending society, the state itself comes to be constituted by a network of power relations between a wide range of constituents. Rather than upholding the law and enforcing it in some neutral way, state officials and actual enforcers of the law selectively intervene, depending on the sense of their own interests and the pressures they take themselves to be under. If government can often convert citizens' rights into a matter for discretion, citizens in turn can often convert law into a matter of convenience. All of this does not result in anarchy, but a politics of countless negotiations. Almost every point where citizens are governed, at every transaction where they are noted, registered, taxed, stamped, licensed, authorized or assessed, the impression of being open for negotiation is given. The actual extent to which enforcement of the law is open for negotiation, bargain or influence, or perverted by corruption, is debatable and hard to assess. But the perception that the affairs of the state are so conducted is widespread. The rule of law is invoked, at best, as a stratagem in such negotiations, not as an instrument of justice. An intricate network of informal loyalties and brokered deals at so many levels of society have ensured that the actions of state towards lawbreaking do not resemble the procedures of a law-abiding society. As a result, the Indian state is often, in day-to-day transactions, neither feared nor loved—incapable of having the rule of law secured either through an effective set of institutions or by eliciting allegiance to its dictates by inspiring a sense of obligation. The state itself has taken on the character of a trading company. Indeed, the efficiency and entrepreneurship with which most public offices have become a means to private gain, might lead one to think that the state has the character of a trading company. Someone once remarked that India runs perfect markets and states; the only trouble is we run a market like the state, and a state like the market.

Given the commanding presence of the state, underwritten by an ideology of state-led development, access to state power became, for good or for ill, the principal means of improving the life chances of individuals. In an economy with slow and sluggish growth, averaging under 3 per cent, the state became a disproportionate provider of opportunity. Even access to opportunities and resources outside the state were mediated through state influence. Indeed, in one sense, politics, through access to state power, became the swiftest route towards social mobility. In a strange kind of way, compared to the market, or educational institutions, politics of all kinds, from the most ambitious aspiration for power to the interest in gaining smallest benefits, came to be seen as a surer way to upward mobility. Access to the state gave jobs and a likely class status that was better than anything available outside the state; the discretionary power the state conferred on all its officials was experienced by many as empowerment, or at least an escape from the subordination that resulted from being at the receiving end of that power. Access to state power was about the only way of ensuring that one counted for somebody. Big scams do not tell the real story of the connection between corruption and social mobility. It is the thousands of petty fortunes that are made through the state that seemed to most citizens a surer bet of improving their class status than the uncertainties of a market. One of the peculiar features of Indian society was that political power became almost the sole means of social mobility. Is there any other sphere of activity that is less stratified and more representative of Indian society than politics?

But the consequence of the growth of the state and its undoubted success in producing a kind of social mobility is attended by a paradox. This paradox is, namely, that once the state is seen as a means for social mobility, it is not, for the most part, seen as the provider of public goods. The state is adjudged to be successful if it can create more opportunities through its own spending, for large numbers of private individuals: if the number of government jobs expands, for instance, even when not required, this is adjudged to be a political success, regardless of the opportunity costs this form of job creation imposes on others. The state exists primarily to satisfy the private interests of collusive interest groups. Although it is undoubtedly true that the dominant proprietary classes will have a disproportionate share of the state's resources, there is enormous fluidity in the nature of social groups that have, at different times, gained access to the state. But the net result has been that almost never has that state been governed by a public philosophy; it is rather a high-stakes competitive game in which individuals or groups seek advantages on particularistic lines. The raison d'être of politics and the aims of public representation are no longer to respond to fundamental issues impinging upon common life but to organize the state's power in such a manner that its resources can be channelled in the direction of particular groups or individuals to protect their exclusive interests. The cumulative impact has been a view of the state and constitutional fabric that see them as institutions to be manipulated according to particularistic interests. One can appropriate Hegel's melodramatic phrase, 'the state exists no longer'. What Hegel meant in his context was that the state and constitution were being manipulated to serve particular interests. The decisions that emanated from it did not carry the necessity of principle, but only the arbitrariness of expedience and hence had little authority. To be sure, there are restraints internal to expedience, but how effective these are will be a matter of some concern. It is extraordinary that the association of the state with the 'public' or the state with the 'common', the two sustaining associations of the state, are wearing so thin.

While the actual achievements of the state are not inconsiderable, a culture of statism did begin to corrode Indian society. Indian politics is dominated by an overwhelming sense that for every shortcoming in society, for every imperfection in its working, for everything left undone, the solution was some form of state action. Slowly and surely, the state came to interpose itself in vast areas of organized life—not just the essentials of security, infrastructure or social and public goods, but almost every single activity was distorted by the imprint of the state. Having divested most other institutions of their enterprise and authority, the state sought to impose its own conception of order, especially on the economy. But the order it sought to impose, even in the heydays of Nehru, lacked any inner momentum; it gave more the appearance of wishful thinking on the part of a small elite trying to create a society in their own image. In practice the state was obliged to accommodate itself to all kinds of groups who were sufficiently willing and able to make their power felt. This only further opened the door to the idea that everything about the Indian state was itself negotiable. Its slender power base exposed, the state took to buying off more and more groups as the price of peace. It shored up its power, not by making itself more effective in its core areas—enforcing rule of law, providing public goods and so on—but by more promiscuous, day-to-day interventions—licences to pursue activities, controls of all kinds, and the distribution of privileges and exemptions by the kind of power most subject to misuse and corruption. Take matters that are relatively peripheral. Art and films were destroyed because the state decided that it was not a legitimate industry, hence they could not raise finance from regular sources; and hence they were delivered over to the underworld. Higher education, where the state has a crucial role to play, and no amount of investment is really enough, was by and large destroyed because in the name of oversight, the state over-regulated this sector in a way in which it was shielded from the imperatives of market forces, and choked much of its creativity. Real estate investment was distorted by the most absurd regulations and control. The whole gamut of activities associated with religion and culture came to be inflected with the imperatives of politics once the state decided that these were within its domain. The cumulative mindset may be described as statism, a syndrome that profoundly influenced the culture of Indian politics.

The net result of statism was that enormous productive energies were enlisted in the struggle to influence government; indeed the very meaning of enterprise became synonymous with the ability to influence government. When the history of Indian entrepreneurship is written, the state will be given its due gratitude. Visit any government office and it is a buzzing den of individuals providing all kinds of services, including those you might have thought to be impossible at a price; by contrast, the hesitations of the members of the Confederation of Indian Industry (CII) about where to next invest, make them almost seem staid by comparison. Certainly, much of Indian industry still struggles with the deep imprint of a political culture where the determinant of success was influence over government rather than enterprise or innovation, and the same instinctive responses came to dominate much other activity, including that of the voluntary sector as well.

The second effect of statism was more subtle: the demand for state intervention became almost compulsively reinforcing. The idea that regulation is the solution to every problem, the idea that regardless of its capacities or interests, the state is the best agency to carry out such regulation, that it is so despite the perverse incentives it is likely to set up, became an almost instinctive political response to any problem. The state itself, meanwhile, had created a set of ruling conventions that were uniquely its own: an almost compulsive and elaborate emphasis on endless formal procedure, each step in the procedure designed to provide oversight to the previous layer of decision-making, without any regard whatsoever for either the opportunity costs involved in such procedures or the outcomes. The state, it seemed, came to inhabit a virtual world of its own, involved in its own language game that after a point did not seem to refer to anything outside of itself. The Indian state almost never evaluated policy by consequences, almost always by its own intent; if the tribunal of its own intentions had been satisfied, nothing else mattered. If it thought rent control helped the poor get housing, or curbs on investment were producing more prosperity, this was so regardless of whether it, in fact, did; particular projects were a success simply because the state had made an allocation for them, not because they reached their intended targets and beneficiaries. The habit of state officials to respond to every query—say why child labour exists—is simply to say that a law exists to deal with the problem. This is not just a last-ditch defensive gesture, it is symptomatic of the way in which the state can become oblivious to the concrete effects of its own action or inaction. The state has internalized the message of the Bhagwad Gita: only intentions and not consequences matter. The net result is that even when policy is not being stymied by the usual combination of vested interests, the state has very little capacity and inclination to carry out careful causal analysis of its own actions. The state's own response to its deficiencies was more of the same: these deficiencies must arise because the state had been lax in regulation.

It is symptomatic that almost every discussion on state reform in India begins with the thought that the state needs more punitive powers.

The state's ability to create an impenetrable world, impervious to outside canons of accountability, has obvious implications for democracy. Partly, the very culture the state fomented, a disregard for the actual consequences of policy, came slowly to penetrate much of our citizens' attitude to policy and shape our expectations as well. If we were candid, we would have to admit that public policy, even in its broad contours, is very poorly discussed, if at all, in the public realm. There is an extraordinary political consciousness about how the state affects the fortune of particular groups, and policy is, therefore, always hostage, as it must be, to countless political negotiations. But whether those negotiations are even minimally informed by general causal considerations about what makes policy sustainable, how competing goals can be reconciled, remains more debatable.

Just like the state is satisfied with its own intent, we are often satisfied with our own. In public debate, this creates the anomaly that we slowly come round to the disposition that there are no facts of the matter, no careful causal analysis—however indeterminate—that can ever be relevant to our own beliefs and dispositions. There is the curious question why policy debate, when it rarely gets conducted in public, is so shrill, drowned out in the end by assertion and counter-assertion. Part of the explanation has got to be that citizens, just like the state, can become impervious to what might be called the 'facts of the matter'. When the debate is simply a clash of intentions, there is no common space that can be occupied to adjudicate and properly debate differences. In the case of citizens who become vocal, public intellectuals and NGOs, this tendency can be reinforced by a real sense of disempowerment. The more you feel distant from a state or institutions, the less implicated you feel in its policies, the more likely you are to be casual in how your policy judgements are formed. And even our intellectuals and policy analysts, who should know better, are often under ideological or other compulsions, less willing to analyse the state in the right terms. Words are often bandied about with zeal, but there referents are not clear. Take, for example, the entire debate over sovereignty and economic policy. Somehow we managed to convince ourselves that government incurring foreign debt was not a sign of dependence, but foreign investment coming in was. We continually confused, and still confuse, legal sovereignty with power, trade with dependence rather than interdependence and so on. The point of this example is not to settle issues of economic policy. The point rather is that our discourse, very much like that of the state, became prisoner of its own good intentions, impervious to refutation or confirmation by the realities we inhabited.

The cumulative result of the way in which the state has come to be perceived has left its imprint on politics. Although democracy has produced an extraordinary amount of churning, the weaknesses of the Indian state have left democracy with few sites where a sense of public purpose can be articulated. Thus arises the central paradox of Indian democracy. Although it has feverishly managed to politicize all social relationships, citizens at the same time are left with a profound sense of disenchantment. Individuals and groups expend inordinate energy to colonize or capture government institutions in seeking to promote their interests over others; there is much activity in politics, but little of it is directed to *public* purposes that all can share.

Non-Deliberative Democracy and the Crisis of Accountability

The disenchantment with the state often expresses itself in the thought that those who wield state power are not accountable. There are few simple formulas for designing accountable institutions, institutions that can be sanctioned in some way to those who authorize them. This is because there is a series of tensions internal to the concept of accountability. The autonomy required for an agency to act properly on our behalf may be impaired by the structure of sanctions we impose upon them. In elections, for example, it is notorious that there is a trade-off between seeing elections as a device to sanction the behaviour of incumbents and seeing them as a screening device for selecting the best candidates. Transparency is sometimes in tension, with responsiveness and representation in tension with both. The crucial point is that harmonizing the different components of accountability cannot be done by conceptual fiat. It is an empirical matter addressed by institutional design and the concrete work of politics. A proper discussion of accountability requires that, at a minimum, attention be paid both to the formal institutional mechanisms by which sanctions *can* be effected and to the collective actions required to ensure that these sanctions *are* effected. The notion of accountability mentioned above raises two sorts of questions: How does the design of institutions provide the *opportunity* to hold policymakers accountable? What are the incentives and mechanisms of accountability? The second sort refers to actions of the principals involved: What are the forms of collective action that are required by citizens to take effective advantage of the *opportunities that institutions offer*? These questions are analytically distinct but related at the same time. Often citizens will not engage in public action if institutions are designed in ways that make their prospects of responding remote. How best to design responsive and accountable institutions is a complex matter that cannot be discussed here. If the Indian state has a weakness, it is this: most of its institutions and rules—courts, bureaucracies, police—are so riddled with perverse incentive structures, that accountability is almost impossible. Most proposals for administrative reform simply add another layer of superintendence to existing institutions without seriously addressing the question why so few in the state, honest or not, act to enhance the accountability of their institutions.

On the other hand, public action outside the formal confines of institutions is, in democracies, at any rate, a significant incentive that shapes institutional behaviour. What politicians think citizens will respond to supposedly has some bearing on their conduct. On what basis is politics conducted in Indian democracy? Many observers of Indian elections find that voters are enormously discerning; no politician or political party can take anything for granted. There are some tangible and sensible ways with which voters measure their well-being: their sense of security for instance; or, as has been demonstrated, high inflation in the year or two immediately preceding an election has serious adverse consequences for the party in power. There is a sense in which India's historical sensitivity to inflation has, so far, placed a serious constraint on the government. But what other expectations, conventions, and hopes does the electorate bring to bear upon politics? Why is there such an extraordinary gap between the discernment of the voters and the outcomes that politics routinely throw up? Why does politics seem either so much about factions' patronage on the one hand and identities on the other. Where is the space for a more sober, practical ideological politics to emerge, where the lines of contestation and difference between political parties, where the culture of political argument is dominated by policy rather than personality, idea rather than faction, and universality rather than identity? What are the obstacles? There is a real sense in which Indian democracy is extraordinarily non-deliberative, especially about policy implications that have a long-term impact.

The reasons for this are complex. In part it has to do with the character of the state itself. The state has arguably never been properly institutionalized as an instrument of common goals. Today it is very difficult for any part to make long-term policy commitments and appear credible. The manner in which economic policy functions in India's electoral process is complex. Probably the single most important puzzle at the heart of any study of accountability in India is the following. Why has India's record at poverty alleviation not been better? Why is there less pressure on the government to deliver a whole range of crucial services like health and education? These two questions are analytically distinct: the first can more readily be explained by poor policy choice; the second demands closer scrutiny. These are compounded by the fact that an old explanation for India's lack of failure in this respect does not hold. This explanation suggests that either the poor do not vote, or some form of coercive or clientelist relationship prevents them from voting on their true preferences. In the Indian case, where there is now reasonably disaggregated data available on voter turnouts, the picture is exactly the opposite of what this explanation hypothesizes. First, the incidence of coercion exercised by local elites in voting matters has gone down significantly, and social relations have been politicized to the extent that old-fashioned clientelist relations are very difficult to sustain. Second, the poor in India have tended to vote more than the middle classes and the rich; rural turnouts are better than urban turnouts, and in recent years, lower and backward castes have voted more than the upper castes. Yet they have not been able to extend concerted public pressure in areas of health and education. One measure of this is captured in government spending statistics on this. In education, the Central and state governments spent 4 per cent of Gross Domestic Product (GDP) for all levels of education in 1996–97 or 13.4 per cent of total government expenditures, which is below the developing country average of 17.5 per cent for all developing countries. India's public spending on health is very low: 1.2 per cent of GDP, which places India amongst the lowest quintile of countries. There is wide variation amongst Indian states on these matters. State expenditures on education, for example, range from 3–7 per cent of Gross State Domestic Product (GSDP) and from 16 to 29 per cent as a share of total state expenditure. The reach of public criticism has been much less effective in Indian democracy when the deprivations people face fall short of the extreme hardships that, say famines, signify. The state's failures in these areas are well known. What is less well understood is the demand side of the equation. Why is political mobilization on *these* issues less effective? Can one just assume that this is simply a product of the *state's* failure, or is there something about the structure and ideologies in civil society that impedes the formation of *effective demand* for health and education?

No political party feels compelled to think that if it suddenly doubled education or health spending as a percentage of GDP, as opposed to introducing more reservations, or engage in paranoid politics of security, it would gain many votes and consolidate a social basis. To be honest, we are not sure what the electoral landholding or distribution of status, are also likely to have the least effective demand for the provision of public goods, as many, including Amartya Sen and Jean Drèze have argued. A society in which citizens do not acknowledge each other is also likely to be a society which cannot get the government to acknowledge them.

But other structural features make government less accountable as well. The first is what might be called the peculiar phenomenon of representation without taxation. Clearly, the vast majority of citizens are in no position to pay taxes of any sort; but a large proportion of those who are—prosperous farmers, professionals, businessmen—pay direct taxes in far lower proportions than they should. In part, this is a consequence of myopic socialist policies in the past that set taxes at such impossibly high levels that tax evasion became an almost institutionalized norm. Take out government employees and the small proportion of labour in the organized sector, and you have virtually a very small base for direct taxes. In effect, private parties stymie the state even before it gets to set policy. To be sure, there is a panoply of indirect taxes, and our collection of taxes over GDP is not as bad as the small base of income-tax payers would suggest. But the net result of this asymmetrical fiscal relationship with the state is this paradoxical attitude towards it: on the one consequences of such a promise, if it appeared credible, would be? But the fact that the entire political class—a class you would trust would be imaginative to be looking for new vote-getting devices—does not think these are credible electoral planks sheds an interesting light on our democracy.

The light it sheds is this: there is little in the citizens' experience of the Indian state that leads them to believe that the state will be a credible provider of social services. In retrospect, one of the great failings of the Nehruvian era, where politics had some credibility, was that between its thwarted ambitions on land reform and its overambitious industrial policy, it left the space for institutionalizing the state as a provider of universal social services relatively open. To be sure, there were serious fiscal and capacity impediments in positioning the state in this way, but the fact that no political party has even tried that is revealing. This has arguably produced a vicious cycle, where because the state has not in the past been an effective provider of health and education, the voters at large do not hold it to account on that score.

What are the obstacles to citizens holding government accountable? The existing inequalities in society, as I have argued, make collective action all that more difficult; states which have the most inegalitarian social structures, either in terms of patterns of hand, because most of us, even the wealthy, do not pay for it, we seem to think that the state is something of a free lunch that anybody can raid without looking at the consequences; the more powerful you are, the better you are in a position to raid it. On the other hand, I suspect that deep down we really don't care about fiscal accountability because we do not have the direct experience for paying for the state. Sure, the middle class does, but much of it is salaried government employees, and the way in which they hold government accountable is by cornering benefits as a pressure group. For them we run a not entirely bad welfare state: the salaried middle classes' relationship to government, demanding benefits in health and education, would be what a classic welfare state with social safety nets would look like. But government employees can garner these only as a pressure group—and they feel entitled because they are the only ones paying! The point is simply this: our fiscal relationship to the state makes most, especially the privileged, relatively uninterested in forms of state spending. The fact that the direct tax base is relatively small means that there will be little cumulative momentum, politically, to monitor the state. It is probably a truism that in most states, the privileged will, on aggregate, garner a disproportionate share of the benefits of the state. But the question is whether their resources can be mobilized to create institutions capable of providing public goods.

This situation is compounded by the fact that the connection between tax collection and spending decisions is organizationally very remote. If voters could discern something of a direct line between their taxes and the benefits they received locally, our politics might be a little more conscious about policy. We are in the worst of both worlds: even when we receive services from the state, we do not see those services as a product of *our* money; and we are fearful that if we pay to the state, the benefits will go elsewhere as it were, not simply to corrupt politicians. The potential benefits of any long-term policy changes are much too uncertain and diffuse. In short, the nature of our fiscal relationship to that state is such that we will not hold it accountable in very general terms.

In principle, both administrative decentralization and devolution of power of the kind envisaged by the 73rd and 74th Amendments to the Constitution and the thrust of Panchayati Raj are meant as an antidote to this kind of centralization. The performance of local bodies such as panchayats and nagarpalikas have been uneven for a variety of complicated reasons, in part because these bodies have simply added a layer of decision-making to other already existing layers, without clearly demarcating lines of authority, in part because existing social inequalities have an adverse impact on the functioning of local government. But one of the reasons is simply that most local bodies still rely too much for grants from other higher-up centralized bodies, and the link between resource generation and expenditure remains unclear. Unless there is a clear and palpable sense that the state is using our resources, we will not hold it to account and that sense has to be made effective through institutions. And this can be done only when to a certain extent we see *our* resources being spent on us in a way in which the line between collection and spending is more direct. To make this link more direct would require radical rethinking in the structure of local government in India.

Overt centralization of governmental functions has long been recognized as the bane of Indian democracy. But one of its consequences is not often remarked upon. And it is that the voters are constantly complaining about the calibre of the political class that has emerged in India; there are constant complaints about its integrity and capacity alike. This complaint can be reformulated in the following terms. We often hear a lament that 'good people' do not enter politics any more. Such a claim is difficult to analyse, in part because the people who are routinely designated as 'bad' or 'just another politician' had the aura of innocence when they first joined. Today's ruling politicians, from the BJP to the Third Front, are a product of the heady idealism that the anti-Emergency and anti-corruption movement produced, and so it is difficult to simply assume that the virtuous shun politics. What is more interesting is whether the virtuous get rewarded for their virtue. I think the short answer is that in the Indian political system individual distinguishing qualities of candidates matter much less than they should, barring cases of exceptional charisma or interest in the qualities of the top leadership. I suggest that this is so for two reasons. First, the obscurity and complexity of most decision-making processes are such that these tend to conceal faults and destroy responsibility. As Alexander Hamilton noted, where there is a plurality of actors, 'the circumstances which may have led to any national miscarriage or misfortunes are sometimes so complicated that though we may clearly see upon the whole that there has been mismanagement, yet it may be impracticable to pronounce on whose account the evil which may have occurred is truly chargeable'. Most Indian voters, especially the educated, are unlikely to pay much attention to the individual records of their representatives, because their accomplishments are difficult to identify as being *their* accomplishments. Only in a structure of government where you can routinely interact with representatives, see them in action, as might be the case if actual power is devolved to smaller local bodies on many issues, are individual characteristics of politicians likely to be more observable. We do not yet have evidence for this, but it is not a wild supposition to assume that the more effectively local institutions function, the more voters will be able to observe the individual distinguishing characteristics of their representatives in those institutions.

Political Parties

The other main obstacle to political accountability is the structure of our political parties. It is a familiar fact that the imperatives of mobilizing funds profoundly influence the politics of almost all parties. But Indian laws on campaign financing—another classic instance of state-led moralism gone awry—have rendered much of the process of election financing non-transparent. Unrealistic spending caps on elections had the perverse effect of making electoral finance more opaque. Rather than ensuring that voters got to know who was getting money from whom through disclosure laws, the entire effort of the state was to wish away expensive elections altogether. This not only generated the need for 'black money', it also distorted the party system. The fragmentation of the party system and the prospect of perpetual coalition governments, the weakening of democratic accountability despite high turnover of incumbents, the fact that political parties are unable to transcend their narrow social bases and become parties of principle, the diminishing quality of public deliberation in our politics—all have their roots, less in the failure of the Constitution than in the party structures that have grown under it. These outcomes are, to a considerable degree, produced by poor institutionalization of intra-party democracy.

The lack of attention given to the inner functioning of political parties is surprising. Most complex democracies are unthinkable without parties. Democracy performs its most salient functions through them. The selection of candidates, the mobilization of the electorate, the formulation of agendas, the passing of legislation—is all conducted through parties. Parties are, in short, the mechanisms through which power is exercised in a democracy. While, thanks to Robert Michels's classic analysis in *Political Parties*, few are naive enough to believe that the oligarchic tendencies of political parties can be entirely overcome, it is abundantly clear that the ways in which parties structure opportunities have decisive outcomes for democracy.

Why does the lack of intra-party democracy produce adverse outcomes for Indian democracy? The poor institutionalization of its procedures means that the internal functioning of parties is not transparent. The criteria for the basic decisions any party has to take, ranging from candidate selection to party platform, remain either unclear or are left to the discretion of one or a handful of leaders. The more the discretionary power vested with leaders, the more a political party will depend solely on its leaders for renewal.

This is so for many reasons. First, one of the most important functions of democracy in any setting is epistemic: to allow the free and uninhibited flow of relevant information. The less internally democratic a party, the less likely it is that the relevant information will flow up party conduits. The Congress leadership's spectacular failure to be attentive to local conditions during the 1970s and 1980s is a recent instance of this phenomenon. Second, if the criteria for advancement within the party are unclear and whimsical, newly mobilized social groups or leaders are less likely to work within existing party structures and will be more tempted to set up their own. If there are no formal mechanisms to challenge entrenched party hierarchies and regulate conflict within parties, they are more likely to fragment.

Kanchan Chandra, for instance, has argued that the relative lack of intra-party democracy within the Congress in UP, compared to that in Karnataka during the 1970s prevented it from incorporating newly mobilized backward-caste groups. Because the criteria for entry and advancement were not clear, these groups were driven to form their own parties rather than take over existing ones. Of course, parties can often incorporate new groups without formally open mechanisms; but such incorporation usually depends upon far-sighted leadership rather than reliable procedures. The lack of such procedures may have contributed to the fragmentation of the party system.

Comparative evidence from Europe and Latin America also suggests that where intra-party democracy is better institutionalized, there is less likely to be this fragmentation. Our fragmented party system may therefore be as much an artefact of the institutional incoherence of our parties as anything else. It is not a coincidence that the evolution of stable party systems and the proper institutionalization of intra-party democracy often go together. Comparative research on Latin America, for example, suggests that reform of the internal functioning of parties was crucial for democratic consolidation in many respects.

It is a notorious fact that Indian democracy is becoming less deliberative in more ways than one can list. Not only are institutions like Parliament rapidly deteriorating in their deliberative capacities and oversight functions, elections also rarely provide an occasion for a protracted wrestling with complex issues. The phenomenon that many observers have described as the 'ethnification' of the party system—whereby voters are most likely to vote according to their caste or some other ethnic affiliation and political parties find it very difficult to transcend their respective social bases—may be in part a product of the fact that elections are rarely a contest of ideas (even if the range is narrow).

If this ethnification is to be overcome, parties will have to ensure that elections are contests over ideas that voters can critically assess. There is a good deal of deserved self-congratulation about the fact that in recent decades Indian democracy has produced an unprecedented mobilization of backward castes and Dalits. But this self-congratulation has occluded the fact that there is relatively little serious, open and protracted discussion of policy issues. Our political parties resist such discussion; most party leaders are unembarrassingly unaware of their own manifestoes; most members of Parliament seem not to have the foggiest idea about the bills they voted for or against; and legislative agendas, with the exception of a few high-profile and often merely symbolic issues, are seldom the object of contention in electoral politics. I cannot see any other way of remedying the lack of public deliberation on these issues other than through changing the culture of political parties in India.

In most democracies, parties perform crucial educative functions. Political leaders used to accepting the discipline and sanctity of democratic procedures within their own parties are also less likely to circumvent democracy when in government. Moreover, protracted intra-party primaries have a profound impact on party members. If the party platform is put up for serious contestation within the party, it is more likely that the members will know why their party takes the positions it does. It is also more likely that the battle within parties will become something more of a battle of ideas rather than a race for patronage.

The simple reason for the poor quality of public deliberation in forums like Parliament is this: the rise of leaders within political parties is not, in a single instance, dependent upon persuading party members of the cogency of your ideas. This is partly a result of the fact that within parties there is no such thing as an open and fair contest at almost any level of the hierarchy. Election campaigns are both too brief and enormous in scope to act as proper forums for protracted deliberation.

In most democracies, the groundwork of political education is done within political parties and the more open and democratic their structure, the more likely it is that politicians will be better educated on the issues. More effective forms of accountability and deliberation require a pluralization of the sites at which politicians are held accountable and parties are essential to this process. The current state of our parties is schooling our politicians in arbitrariness, haphazardness, uncertainty and lack of deliberative purpose.

Poorly institutionalized intra-party democracy produces more factions. In circumstances where the legitimacy of contending groups within a party is not dependent upon a clearly verifiable and open mandate from within the party, the survival of political leaders depends more on political intrigue than on persuading their followers. And those who lose out in this process can nurse the illusion that they were victims of intrigue rather than of their own failures.

Hence, those who lose the contest for party leadership are never delegitimized. Only in a system where the road to the top is less dependent upon creating a mass support within the party can so many politicians openly harbour the ambition of the highest office. Of course, much factionalism is simply a product of ambition. But ambition is given freer rein in circumstances where there are no settled procedures to determine whose authority counts.

All our political parties are in internal disarray. The Congress has no institutional mechanisms for incorporating new groups or generating a set of leaders with some popular base or having an open discussion of ideas. Even within the BJP, there is a potential war of succession. The Third Front has always been hampered by the fact that there are no clear criteria to determine who will inherit the mantle of leadership. The only way in which this Front can coalesce into an enduring coalition is if it can settle upon procedural norms that will facilitate decisions rather than rely upon the whims and ambitions of a handful of leaders. In the absence of clear democratic procedures within the parties to resolve these questions, these parties will continue to be plagued by the factionalism that has been so detrimental to both their own interests and the stabilization of the party system.

The simple fact is that the lack of intra-party democracy impedes proper representation rather than enhancing it. By their non-transparency, parties have restricted voter choices rather than increasing them. The reasons for this lack are not hard to understand. Parties are endogenous institutions that adopt certain norms and procedures. The question is under what conditions do parties choose to create democratic rules and procedures in the first place? What incentives do they have to institutionalize democracy within their parties?

Here, the answers turn out not to be very encouraging. Leaders like as much control over their parties as possible. They like to set agendas, select candidates that are beholden to them, and maintain themselves in power. Most leaders have an incentive not to institutionalize settled procedures for challenging their power. And those who are left out of power circuits within parties find it difficult to act collectively to reform procedures.

This is so for a number of reasons. They can be individually bought off by those in power; they fear the added uncertainty to their prospects for advancement that contesting elections might create; and few have enough commitment to procedural proprieties to fight for them. The short-term interests of party leaders are thus often at odds with the long-term interests of the party. But unless political parties themselves provide opportunities for regular and open and fair contests, Indian politics is likely to remain undeliberative.

Ideological Stalemate

Indian democracy is in a vicious deadlock. There is no sustained ideological conception of the state as an instrument for delivering services that should be open to all. Thus the state is judged on a very narrow range of policy issues, perhaps inflation and corruption but little else. All the institutional structures impede the creation of a more deliberative politics. Political parties, as I had suggested, do so by being deliberately under-institutionalized; the fact that the state is so centralized and remote makes it hard to figure out individual lines of accountability. Inter-temporal accountability mechanisms are very weak because the effects of policy decisions that are likely to have an enduring impact for the better—reallocation of budgetary priorities, capital investment, yield results too late for most incumbents to benefit. Most voters judge the impact of policies on their well-being, not by the *future* aggregate impact these policies are likely to have on them, but on their immediate benefits. In many candid conversations with politicians, they will readily admit that in their assessment greater spending on schools and hospitals, on investment, usually will not yield returns before the next election.

Cumulatively, therefore, most politicians are in search for consolidating constituencies through one of two methods: either short-term handouts, or searching for some symbolic issues that can draw together constituencies of voters. Long-term projects such as infrastructure projects do matter to politicians, but less because they are confident that these have immediate electoral payoffs. Often such projects are the source of immense rents; often they are attractive because they are the means through which the state can present itself as a spectacle. Thus politicians have a great preference for direct methods of poverty alleviation. Direct transfers of money are more amenable to pilferage, to not put too fine a point on it, they are administratively easier and quicker to enact than long-term projects that might bring about enduring change, and they can be targeted more according to the discretion of politicians. It has also been shown, for instance, that there is a very direct link between increases in subsidies and electoral cycles; and routinely governments will hand out 'freebies' such as forgiven loans, written off bills, pay awards. The kinds of pressures that have been brought to bear through the franchise suggest that *immediate* benefits are electorally more salient than long-time horizon changes.

But there is only so much by way of a constituency that you can forge through short-term state handouts. Most of these discretionary goodies will be cornered by powerful constituencies; and traditional wisdom has it that a collusion of prosperous farmers, public sector employees, industrial capitalists, and a privileged sector of organized labour exercised an effective lock on government policy. None of these classes was powerful enough to dominate the state on their own, while their combined fears about the consequences of altering state policy meant that long-term changes in government's priorities was often structurally inhibited. This account could vastly exaggerate the hold dominant classes have on the state, and underestimate the room politicians have for manoeuvre.

So how do politicians then carve out major electoral coalitions? The politics of identity is a natural candidate. It has the advantage of linking large numbers of constituents in webs of interest, identification and affiliation in a way in which talk of 'common' interests, as in shared universal entitlements, does not. Of course, the politics of identity does not operate in a vacuum, independently of other interests. But its attraction in a polity, marked, as I have already argued, by a great crisis of self-esteem and competitive group relations is enormous, even though its limitations remain palpable.

At this historical juncture, one gets the overwhelming feeling that Indian politics is characterized by an ideological decadence. It would be difficult to find a label or a slogan that can capture the meaning of contemporary Indian politics in any significant way. One would be even more hard-pressed to find a label that can capture and name the energies that are driving it and the goals that are inspiring it. It appears that the best one can do is to describe our politics as a stalemate politics: a politics that is too vacuous even to give itself a name.

To be sure, there is, to borrow a sentence from Aurobindo, an impotent and sterilizing chaos of names, labels, programmes and war cries. Cultural nationalism, agrarian protests, Dalit assertion, minority discontent, environmental energies, anti-globalization sentiments, pro-liberalization flamboyance, all dot our political landscape. All lift the banner of conflicting ideals, and some even have worthy causes attached to them. But mostly they are unable to escape the damaging suspicion that under the flag of ideals, all that is really going on is a battle of conflicting interests. They may energize this or that group for sporadic action, but are unable to mobilize sustainable moral energies. While Hindu nationalism remains a menace, even its adherents are so cynical about its uses that its status as a genuine artefact of belief remains doubtful. The churning of Indian politics and society that followed Mandal has petered out into an endlessly involuted conflict of one sub-caste with another. Most anti-caste movements turn out, on inspection, to be merely anti-upper-caste movements, quite happy to exclude those below them. The government is embarked on radically restructuring the Indian economy, yet it does it so haltingly that it appears nothing more than a counsel of despair. Anti-globalization thinking is too happy just being 'anti' something to be constructive.

One could argue that the vacuity of ideology is an opportune moment for a pragmatic orientation to politics. It allows space for constructive and manageable tasks like building infrastructure, schools and hospitals, securing the food supply, managing the environment, without the dogmatic encumbrances of ideology. There are many ongoing efforts in this direction. But these seldom give politics a direction. And current circumstances induce a paralysis even into these efforts. Responsible and well-meaning citizens blame the World Trade Organization (WTO) for starvation deaths, globalization for poor public health and America for our poor infrastructure, forgetting the fact that there is nothing preventing our state from addressing these problems if it and we all wanted to address them. It is not that the enduring sources of ideological conflict have disappeared. The perpetual struggle between the privileged and the dispossessed, the anxieties about being able to collectively define our own destinies, the two most enduring sources of political energy, remain. But they cannot cohere on any articulate lines. To descend into the ideological world of Indian politics is to descend not into the placid consensus of a post-ideological age, but into a chaos of a world that is struggling to interpret its own meaning. All the ruling ideas of our politics are burdened with so many limitations and disclaimers that they are unable to give the world any degree of coherence and provide a source of moral conviction. Is this a purely transitory phase?

It has become fashionable in some circles to argue that increasing globalization and liberalization of the economy have rendered redistributive politics irrelevant. On this view, the growth generated by economic reforms will by itself be sufficient to lift significant sections of society out of poverty. Whatever the intentions, the net effect of a redistributive politics in the Indian case is increased statism and regulation. Since dominance of the state dampened innovation, circumscribed entrepreneurship, stifled growth and prevented living standards from rising, undue emphasis on redistribution, is likely to hamper growth.

This argument derives its plausibility from two fallacies that underlay previous paradigms of redistributive politics in India. First, by and large, those on the left who advocated redistribution failed to give adequate recognition to the importance of economic growth. Second, the call for a redistributive politics was often confused between two different aims: poverty alleviation and economic equality. In principle, the two are distinct. Prosperity and inequality can coexist as much as poverty and greater equality. The Indian left's suspicion of the market has predominantly been derived from a fear of inequality. To put it bluntly, the Indian left minded inequality more than it did poverty.

Only the most dogmatic of ideologues can deny that the growth generated by the reform process started in the 1990s has brought substantial gains. This growth has lifted close to tens of millions of people above the poverty line and created a substantial middle class. It is probably fair to say that this growth has benefited the upper half amongst those below the poverty line more than it has benefited the most abject of the poor. For the most abject of the poor, state policy will continue to be important, though frankly, the state has very little political incentive to take them seriously. They are also likely to be the group least acknowledged by other citizens as an object of concern. At least in the southern and western states, growth also seems to have had a beneficial impact on human development indicators. Yet these developments and the past fallacies of the redistributive paradigms do not render the politics of economic justice irrelevant.

What paradigm should a new politics of redistribution take? There is a considerable irony underlying past paradigms of redistributive politics. The Indian left, for instance, produced some of the most incisive analysis of the ways in which the Indian state came to be captured by dominant proprietary classes. Yet, what was its solution to this problem? Invest even more hopes and resources in the very state that it had declared to be thoroughly captured by the dominant classes in the first place. The second paradigm of redistributive politics was based on the idea that access to state power would empower marginalized groups like the lower and backward castes. This argument has considerable merit but is limited in its scope. The state has limited resources, its capacities for expansion are at breaking point, and most wealth in society will be generated outside the state. While most of the middle classes were using the best private and foreign institutions available to get access to the leading sectors of the economy, members of marginalized groups were being condemned to second-rate institutions.

It is very clear that these two paradigms of a redistributive politics, increasing power of the state, or redistribution through increased state spending, are currently unviable. The great disjuncture in Indian politics consists of the fact that all the distributional coalitions are still based on old redistributive paradigms. The left's reflexes are limited to a kind of statism that protects the state sector even if it means stifling the rest of the economy. Caste politics after Mandal has not generated new ideas that can bring about a significant transformation. The proponents of both paradigms fear that reforming the state will have a disproportionate impact on parts of their key constituencies. The left wants to protect labour in the state sector at the expense of economic growth; the proponents of Mandal fear that rolling back the state just at the moment at which Backward Castes are getting access to its resources would be an exercise in bad faith. The proponents of both have been unable to articulate a different paradigm of distributional politics. In practice, of course, they are more pragmatic. Even though, when in Opposition, all political parties have conspired to slow down the process of economic reform, they become reluctant liberalizers when in power. But this impetus towards liberalization is still largely driven by the exigencies of fiscal crisis, rather than any long-term strategic vision. On the other side, proponents of reform have been unable to build a new political constituency by showing the ways in which economic reform can be used to empower marginalized groups in Indian society. This is so for a number of reasons. First, the capacity to generate economic growth is not by itself a winning political strategy. In India, political parties routinely lose elections in periods of high growth. Political coalitions cannot be created and sustained around the slogan of 'growth' in the way in which they can be around distribution. The gains of growth, while tangible, are diffuse and indirect and it is more difficult to claim causal responsibility for them. Second, proponents of liberalization have not come up with imaginative ways in which they can show a direct link between the process of economic liberalization and distributional gains for the newly influential groups in politics like the backward castes. The fact that no political party has managed to use the process of economic liberalization to form a new distributional coalition has meant that the process of reform continues to be slow, piecemeal and uncertain. While there may even be a policy consensus on the desirability of reforms, there is no distributional coalition sustaining them.

Can the process of economic reform be linked to a new kind of distributional aspiration? Such a link is quite necessary to sustain the political credibility and legitimacy of economic reform. Early proponents of markets like Adam Smith knew fully well that markets as institutions can be legitimized only if they are allied with a redistributive politics that brought gains to all sections of society. While growth would be necessary for lifting people out of poverty, it would by no means be sufficient.

For one thing, the state would have to create the social preconditions for a successful market economy. Proponents of economic liberalization have been presumptuously silent about how these preconditions are to be created. How will marginalized groups, which form the basis of appeals to a distributional politics, be given proper access to make full use of the opportunities of the market? The left, on the other hand, has tried to avoid this question by in effect becoming the party that protects the Indian state, as it is currently constituted. The crafting of a new distributional coalition now depends upon thinking of imaginative ways in which the state can be used to help more people gain access to these opportunities. One modest proposal would go as follows.

There is a legitimate fear that the proceeds that accrue to the state from liberalization will not be

123

invested in the creation of an infrastructure that will ensure that marginalized groups can fully benefit from the opportunities of a market economy. The simple solution to this fear is to earmark all the funds generated from disinvestments for programmes that will help these groups gain access to the market economy. The purpose of this earmarking would be to use these funds to help Dalits and other marginalized groups gain access to the market economy in much the same way in which affirmative action ensured access to the state. This can be done in a variety of ways: investment in education, ensuring that the groups have the same access to those private institutions that are increasingly the gateway to the market economy, creating a class of Dalit entrepreneurs in much the same way as we have created a class of Dalit civil servants, and so on. The simple fact is that the interests of these groups will, in the long run, be better served by access to the private sector where most future wealth is likely to be generated; and the process of reforms will gain greater legitimacy if a direct link can be established between liberalization and gains for marginalized groups. No liberal polity can be stable or its collective life free of destructive communal conflict so long as most people lack the minimum resources for independence and social self-respect. The politics of liberalization has come in fits and starts, as a manoeuvre amongst shifting elites, but without much electoral appeal, because it has not made its redistributive consequences clear. We are faced with a stalemate: a statism that is fiscally unsustainable, morally corrupting and political corrosive on the one hand, and an anti-statism that has no social coalition behind it, whose consequences most people feel are uncertain, and one that needs the state to legitimize it on the other. We need to give marginalized groups a stake in the reform process; it would break the reflexive statism that dominates left politics, and it would create a new distributional coalition to sustain reforms. The challenge is to make populism and the market work for each other, rather than against one another.

In short, critics of the state, the defenders of individual enterprise, those who have great faith that the choices people will make, if left to their own devices, will result in benefits for all, will need to understand that a polity will not be stable, nor its life free of destructive communal conflict, if the vast majority of the population languishes without assets or opportunities. Private initiative can generate wealth, but well-functioning state institutions will be, at times, indispensable in assuring that these gains can be translated into genuine assets and opportunities for all. Public institutions are also required for civic purposes, to define a space of mutual acknowledgement and reciprocity rather than domination and competition. A society with no shared public philosophy in which all its citizens have a stake is not likely to be a society with capacities for sustainable collective action. On the other hand, we have to recognize that the state cannot be fetishized as an end in itself, that if it seeks to supplant individual choice and initiative, it will end up being corrupt and corrosive and undermine its own effectiveness.

What Indian democracy needs is a new sense of the relationship between public and private: recognizing that there are some things states are particularly bad at, but also recognizing that we will be impoverished unless all enjoy the minimum bases for social self-respect and acknowledge each other through projects we hold in common. The protection of individual liberty so that each one of us can realize ourselves, in our own way, the provision of security, in the wider sense of the term, and the expansion of economic opportunity are perhaps the most substantive ways of creating a social world that is habitable for all. This will require an extraordinary effort on so many different fronts, but understanding the complexity of the task will put us in a far better position to cope with our social world than the politics of illusion that our political parties offer. Genuine politics is nothing, if not, in Max Weber's memorable words, the 'slow boring of hard boards'. The peculiar dignity of democracy is that at least it gives us an opportunity to try, to exercise our *choices* as citizens.

ACKNOWLEDGEMENTS

Even a small book such as this is not possible without great support. I am profoundly grateful to:

The editors at the *Telegraph* and *The Hindu* for giving me such extraordinary support and their commitment to enhancing the quality of public deliberation; to the editors at the *Indian Express* for encouraging the agonistic spirit democracy needs. In particular, I owe a debt to my friend Rudrangshu Mukherjee, whose indulgence and support have encouraged my writing, and N. Ravi for inviting me to contribute to *The Hindu*.

Kamini Mahadevan at Penguin Books, for her intellectual inventiveness and support for authors; to Sakshi Narang, for making this essay vastly more intelligible than it was when Penguin first received it.

Michael Sandel for insisting that democracy can use idealism; Richard Tuck and Istvan Hont for their defence of 'realism'.

Alan Ryan and George Kateb, exemplary liberals and teachers.

Devesh Kapur, Glyn Morgan and Russ Muirhead for an incessant flow of ideas and for the democratic virtues of independence, iconoclasm, irreverence and friendship.

My family, robust, combative and democratic individualists all, and to whom this book is dedicated.

YOU MAY ALSO LIKE

India's Legal System: Can It Be Saved?
Fali S. Nariman

An incisive and comprehensive view of India's legal process and its key issues

India has the second-largest legal profession in the world, but the systemic delays and chronic impediments of its judicial system inspire little confidence in the common person. In India's Legal System, renowned constitutional expert and senior Supreme Court lawyer Fali S. Nariman explores the possible reasons. While realistically appraising the criminal justice system and the performance of legal practitioners, he elaborates on the different aspects of contemporary practice, such as public interest litigation, judicial review and activism. In lucid, accessible language, Nariman discusses key social issues such as inequality and affirmative action, providing real cases as illustrations of the on-ground situation.

This frank and thought-provoking book offers valuable insights into India's judicial system and maps a possible road ahead to make justice available to all.

YOU MAY ALSO LIKE

Secular Common Sense
Mukul Kesavan

In this essay, Kesavan argues that secularism is (and has always been) the political common sense of the Republic. Before Independence, secularism grew out of the necessary pluralism of Congress politics. The Congress was inclusive because it had to prove to a sceptical colonial State that it genuinely represented the diversity of India. After Independence and the traumas of Partition, the function of Nehruvian secularism was to reassure Indians of every sort that they lived in the Republic by right and not on sufferance. Secularism became a way of making the republican State credible to all its constituents.

For Kesavan, republican secularism is not a radical cause. As written into India's Constitution, secularism has had a single, simple aim: it has tried to make sure that no one community monopolizes the State and its institutions. Hindutva threatens this foundational safeguard because it claims the State in the name of a single community. It represents in politics a monopolistic take-over bid, a coup in slow motion. It should be opposed because it wants to replace the secular common sense of our Republic with the rhetoric of grievance and resentment.

YOU MAY ALSO LIKE

*The Case That Shook India: The Verdict That Led to
the Emergency*
Prashant Bhushan

**The only account of the landmark case that
disqualified Indira Gandhi as PM**

On 12 June 1975, for the first time in independent India's
history, the election of a Prime Minister was set aside by a
High Court judgment. The watershed case, Indira Gandhi
v. Raj Narain, acted as the catalyst for the imposition
of the Emergency. Based on detailed notes of the court
proceedings, *The Case That Shook India* is both a legal and a
historical document of a case that decisively shaped India's
political destiny.

The author, advocate Prashant Bhushan, sets out to reveal
the goings-on inside the court as well as the manoeuvrings
outside it, including threats, bribes and deceit. Providing
a blow-by-blow account, he vividly recreates courtroom
scenes. As the case goes to the Supreme Court, we see how
a ruling government can misuse legislative power to save
the PM's election.

Through his forceful and gripping narrative, Bhushan
offers the reader a front-row seat to watch one of India's
most important legal dramas unfold.